P<small>RAISE FOR</small>

MESSAGES FROM THE LIGHT

"Each of us gets to face death. NDErs help us to better understand and not fear it. Getting wisdom and advice from the other side is comforting, insightful, helpful, and meaningful. All this is packaged here for you."

~**Mark Victor Hansen,** co-creator, #1 *New York Times* best-selling series *Chicken Soup for the Soul* and coauthor, *Cracking the Millionaire Code*

"Christophor Coppes has been deeply touched by near-death experiencers and what they say, so much so that it has altered how he views the world. As a world-class economist, he has a fresh perspective that is worth reading."

~**P.M.H. Atwater,** LHD, near-death researcher, and author of *The Big Book of Near-Death Experiences*

"*Messages From the Light* by Christophor Coppes is an important book that everyone should read. *Messages From the Light* provides not only detailed reports from hundreds of people who have had near-death experiences, but gives the context on why such experiences occur, and the deeper messages that are being conveyed not just to those who experience near-death, but to all of us, whatever our personal belief system. We are living in a critical era in which our every thought and action has the potential to direct human destiny, either in a positive or negative direction. *Messages From the Light* has the ability to inspire each of us toward the positive."

~**William Gladstone,** international best-selling author of *The Twelve*

"This well-written and interesting book is not just about NDEs, but especially focuses on the impressive changes in life insight that usually follow an NDE. We can all learn from these messages from the light because we desperately need to change our worldview before it is too late. We have to respect each other, and should no longer exploit the natural resources of our planet, because everybody and everything seems to be eternally interconnected in a kind of unity universe, which makes it possible to have influence on all there is. This change in personal consciousness becomes possible by listening with an open mind to the messages that people with an NDE share with us in this inspiring book."

~Pim van Lommel, cardiologist, author of *Consciousness Beyond Life*

"While reading *Messages from the Light*, I was highly impressed with how Christophor Coppes has knit together his many years of NDE research, knowledge, and own intuitive insights...all into one book. This book is filled with fascinating perspective, and I suspect most readers will walk away feeling richer for having read it!"

~Christian Andréason, award-winning recording artist and singer

Messages From the Light

MESSAGES FROM THE LIGHT

True Stories of Near-Death Experiences and Communication From the Other Side

BY CHRISTOPHOR COPPES

NEW PAGE BOOKS
A division of The Career Press, Inc.
Pompton Plains, NJ

MESSAGES FROM THE LIGHT
EDITED AND TYPESET BY NICOLE DEFELICE
Cover design by Ian Shimkoviak/The Book Designers
Printed in the U.S.A.

To order this title, please call toll-free 1-800-CAREER-1 (NJ and Canada: 201-848-0310) to order using VISA or MasterCard, or for further information on books from Career Press.

The Career Press, Inc.
220 West Parkway, Unit 12
Pompton Plains, NJ 07444
www.careerpress.com
www.newpagebooks.com

Library of Congress Cataloging-in-Publication Data
Coppes, Christophor.
    Messages from the Light : the stories of near-death experiences and communication from the other side / by Christophor Coppes.
        p. cm.
Includes bibliographical references (p.) and index.
ISBN 978-1-60163-138-1 -- ISBN 978-1-60163-689-8 (ebook) 1. Near-death experiences. I Title.

BF1045.N4C65 2011
133.901'3--dc22

                                                                    2010034224

I would like to dedicate this book to the many Near-Death Experiencers (NDErs) to whom I spoke. They made a difference in my life. They led me in the right direction, and let me into the wonderful messages that they had during their Near-Death Experiences (NDEs). I noticed how deeply they were affected by their experience, so much so, that they need a lot of time to adapt to our "earthly" way of life again. That is why I thought of asking seasoned NDErs what advice they have for recent NDErs and, as a form of gratitude, put that advice in the closing chapter. And the nicest thing about this advice is that it is valuable not only to NDErs, but to other people as well.

Near-Death Experience

I touched the universe
I was in the fifth dimension
in the implicate order
I felt unconditional love
light, lightspeed
and infinity
while meditating
I felt, saw and heard
in the silence
between my thoughts
that same fifth dimension
of unconditional love
and infinity
I experienced
that life and death
exists in the duality
of the fourth dimension
the dimension of space and time
and that the spirit
of unconditional love
light, lightspeed
and infinity
exists in the fifth dimension
of the implicate order
of the universe

~FRANS TOMEIJ[1]

CONTENTS

PREFACE

When we see the colors of the rainbow we actually see divided light. Each color is separated light. Yet, each color is beautiful on its own, and beautiful when seen with shades of the same color, or even with stark contrasting colors. All of them are important, not only because they can form wonderful pictures, but also because they come from the same source. When they are put together, each will disappear and they will form white light again.

We can see ourselves and the whole world we live in as a rainbow: We are multiple colors. We get our specific color from being separated from the Light source. That, in itself, makes every single one of us extremely important. There are no lesser souls. In addition, we have the ability to create beautiful pictures together. But the most important thing is to realize that together we are one, forming one big, brilliant light.

This book tries to make that clear. We participate in an enormous unity universe, of which we only see a fraction. Even though we seem insignificantly small, each of us is indispensable, because we are ingeniously interconnected with everyone and everything there is. Through this interconnection, we have influence on everything. This is our creative part, which we can use to add energy to the world, but also to freeze energy. When we see a great deal of the freezing of energy, it is the consequence of our focus on short-term self-interest. Nevertheless, we will learn from the consequences, we will change, and we will see a better world emerge when we realize that we have to focus on long-term "our-interest." To make this happen, it would be best for us to use our free will to become aligned with The Light.

The idea that it is best for us to align with The Light is based on the messages from many Near-Death Experiencers. So, my tribute is to them. They had experiences that they often characterize as marvelous and extremely valuable, which they cherish throughout the rest of their lives as if it were a treasure, but which also rigorously threw them off their feet and thoroughly changed their lives. It cost them a great deal of energy to cope with their mind-blowing experiences. Their experiences not only made a difference in their lives, but also in mine, and hopefully in those of many others.

In this book, I follow a specific argument, which I gradually developed through the many interviews I had with NDErs. It is also based on NDE-accounts written in other publications, such as books, specialized magazines, and the scientific *Journal of Near-Death Studies.* I discovered recurring themes in NDEs, which I use to set up my argumentation. Of particular importance was an interview with a woman who was able to tell me in advance that the financial and economic crisis was going to aggravate seriously. Many other NDErs support the argument that I developed from this and other interviews.

To illustrate the themes and to support my argument, I use carefully chosen quotes from interviewees and publications. I love these quotes because they clearly describe the essentials of the relevant theme. I could never describe the theme so well as the particular NDEr did.

In a few cases, the quotes come from the experiences submitted anonymously to the archives of IANDS. In all cases, names and identifying details have been changed to protect privacy except for those who explicitly allowed me to use their name. Should any of the anonymous contributors to the International Association for Near-Death Studies (IANDS) archives like to be made known, they can contact me through the publisher or through my Website: *www.christophor.nl.* I was not able to obtain their identity, because understandably IANDS needs to keep the identity of the anonymous contributors secret.

When, after reading this book, your curiosity about these experiences is aroused and you still want to know more about them, I would like to recommend the official Website of the International Association of Near-Death Studies: *www.IANDS.org*. There you will find recommended reading, an archive of many experiences and links to IANDS groups around the world, including the United States. The network in the Netherlands is Merkawah, of which I am president. Another interesting Website with an NDE-archive is *www.nderf.org*. And in case you would like to know more about me and my previous books, go to *www.christophor.nl.*

Finally, I want to thank Rose Divito, Tom Bagguley, and Julia Park for their help with improving the English text.

Chapter 1

Increase Our Spiritual Wealth

We are on a dead-end street and we have to turn around. For too long, our focus has been on our own short-term self-interest and by doing this we created an I-don'-care-about-you society. We have to take the next step in our development: focusing on our long-term "our-interest." The financial crisis will help us change, and though it will be a painful process, we are destined for a more wonderful world, materially as well as spiritually.

Positive ripples

What do a gorilla and Near-Death Experiencers (NDErs) have in common? Not much I would think, but I need them both to know how important it is to become aligned with The Light, and to create as many positive ripples as we can.

The Gorilla was his nickname for being the ruthless archetypal banker. He was the last boss from Lehman Brothers. Just before his firm went belly-up, two top managers were awarded bonuses of several millions, and later in a court hearing, he would declare that the $350 million he earned in the 10 years of heading his company were appropriate. For years, he had been proud of having one of the top 10 incomes on Wall Street. One year, he discovered that his name was not on the list, and it upset him terribly.

The default of his firm ignited the current financial and economic crisis, which is nowadays called the Great Recession but which seemed more like a "Great Implosion" of the financial system.[1] A total destruction could only be avoided by the hasty but massive financial rescue by governments and central banks around the world. They pumped hundreds of billions of dollars into the system. But, just after their rescue with taxpayers' money, Wall Street and London bankers again awarded themselves tens of billions of dollars in bonuses.

Nothing is wrong with bankers (I am in banking myself), nor is there anything wrong with money or with earning money, even when it is a lot. Money is a wonderful thing; it is a sort of energy that can be used to create, to do something productive, and thus to add something positive to our world. However, the previous examples show that, for some people, money has become the goal and everything else was made subordinate to acquiring it. Why else would someone feel terribly upset while sitting on a heap of millions?

This attitude toward money is not something exclusive to some bankers. It is something that became a standard practice for many people. Take for instance the British members of Parliament who seem to be so "honorable." They turned out to be barefaced profiteers. Remember that they were claiming expenses for many things that were not really work-related, while, in the end, the taxpayers footed the bill. Items such as dog food, diapers, toilet seats, porn movies, the repair of a drainage system of a private tennis lawn, and even the purchase of a floating duck house were on the list. Did they think these were very essential to perform their parliamentary duties?

Here is an example from the judiciary of this twisted attitude toward money. For many years the privatized youth detention center in Pittston paid two judges in Wilkes-Barre, Pennsylvania, for delivering detainees. One of the co-owners of the prisons confessed to the FBI that he paid the judges for high sentences. It is estimated that some 5,000 young people were thrown into prison wrongfully, or have received too high a sentence for only minor offences. Total earnings for this kind of trafficking of children: about $ 2.6 million. Total damage to the lives of these adolescents: immeasurable.

Admittedly, these examples are excessive, but they demonstrate the ego-centered intentions. If we are honest, we might also come up with some examples, albeit less extreme, where we could question our own intentions. I need stories of NDErs to make sufficiently clear why intentions have an impact on the world, and why the lack of good intentions has brought us this Great Recession.

This book is about the importance of intentions, about the ripples they create, and how they vibrate throughout the world. It discusses how positive intentions create positive ripples, and negative intentions create negative ones. It argues that the purpose of life, despite all its problems and setbacks, is to expand our ability to love. It will be stressed that we have focused for too long on our financial wealth, and too little on our spiritual wealth. The book will offer a non-economic explanation of the Great Recession and urges us to learn from it quickly.

The conclusion is that we are on a dead-end street. We have to turn around. We have focused on our own short-term self-interest for too long, and by doing this, we have created an I-don't-care-about-you society. True, self-interest has helped us to create a prosperous society, but we really have to take that next step toward long-term "our-interest." If we don't, then our selfish attitude will will bring us down and cause us to fall back. We will reap what we have sown: the ripples that we created with our egoism. And if we create enough negative ripples, they will turn into unavoidable tsunamis, not only financially, but also environmentally. It was stressed by some NDErs that the Great Recession will be nothing compared to the environmental crises we are slowly running into. We will perish in a climate that has derailed and turned hostile due to our own interference. We will experience shortages in food and water; we will have renewed financial and economic shocks. It is bound to be our outcome if we don't quickly change our attitudes.

The good news is that we will change. We are destined to do so, but that doesn't mean that we can sit down and wait passively. If we do, we will surely experience more of these shocks. Therefore, we have to work hard to avoid them, and though it will be a painful process, we will then see the dawn of a less selfish world, which, of course, is a tremendous reward.

The source is Near-Death Experiences

The source for arriving at these truths is extraordinary experiences from ordinary people. These are the people who have had a Near-Death Experience (NDE). They come from many walks of life: they are male or female, young or old, doctors, bankers, artists—you name it. They are so very important, because they are absolutely convinced that during their experience they have had a brief glimpse of heaven. For me, they form an indirect peephole through which we can acquire some insight into the meaning of creation and the purpose of our lives. For that reason, I have spent a lot of time studying these experiences and had a lot of interviews with NDErs. I am convinced that what they say is true and in Chapter 2, I will explain why.

I wanted to listen only to them and to hear only their messages. I didn't want to listen to religious people or people with psychic powers. It's not that I don't believe them, but I wanted to go to the purest source. These are the many different ordinary people who have had an NDE and, therefore, have been in heaven, or at least on its doorstep, for a brief moment. They do not change their original story. They stick to it, even decades after their experience. Their message is original. They don't mix it with new ideas or change their message as they go through life. They maintain that here on earth, we live in a surrogate reality, while what they have experienced over there is the real thing. It is more real than everyday life.

Perhaps you will say that NDEs are nonsense. They are caused by a lack of oxygen or by other chemical reactions or neurological processes in the brains of a dying patient. I could point to fine research, acknowledged by mainstream science, that shows that these do not cause NDEs (see Chapter 2). You would perhaps tell me that still, no one knows the real reason why NDEs occur, and I would have to admit that point. But, then I could tell you the stories of people who were able to wander around their hospital room or who could clearly see what happened during their own operation, while being clinically dead. They have been out of their bodies and discovered that they still had clear consciousness. There are some strong, well-documented cases for the ability of our consciousness to be independent from our physical body, to wander around and make specific observations that could later be confirmed (the so-called veridical observations).

In addition, there are many people who had a meaningful communication during their NDE about what they were going to experience later in their lives. What they saw would turn out to make perfect sense at that point later in their life. For instance, one of these people had seen the Great Recession evolving after Lehman's bankruptcy, which severely shook the whole financial world. She had told me about it months before it actually happened (see Chapter 8).

Veridical observations while being out of their body, plus the meaningful communication, seem to prove what man has always believed throughout history: Life doesn't stop with death. NDEs seem to demonstrate that our consciousness is eternal.

Perhaps you would say that all these stories are ridiculous and unbelievable. The mere fact that stories seem unbelievable in the world as we know it doesn't mean that they are untrue. Remember what happened to Marco Polo, who set out for China in 1271, when he was about 19 years old. He was among the first representatives of a European civilization who became acquainted with the much more ancient (and then still mysterious) Chinese civilization. It turned out to be a culture shock. At that time, much of what he saw was unknown in his hometown of Venice.

In China, he was received with great honor by emperor Kublai Khan. He described how powerful and wealthy the emperor was. For instance, he issued money made of paper, which was stamped with the imperial seal. To Marco's astonishment, it was being accepted in exchange for valuable things, such as pearls, jewels, gold, silver, or any other product. Counterfeiting was a capital punishment. The first European bank notes did not occur until 1661 in Sweden and 1691 in England!

In China, glass turned out to be used by people to see well. Eating habits were totally different. For instance, they ate ice cream, which was unknown in Europe at that time. Wine was made from rice, which for Europeans, who only knew wine made from grapes, must have sounded very strange, indeed.

He was astonished by the immense population. The peculiar thing about these people was that, when it was within reach, they took three baths a week, and in the winter, they bathed every day. Every man of rank or wealth had his own bath in his house. Heating all the stoves and baths would take too much wood, but fortunately there was a province where black stone was dug out of the mountains. It burned like charcoal when lit, and retained the fire much better than wood. In Europe, coal was unknown at that time, and the idea of stones burning was unheard of.

At that time in Europe, people were absolutely fascinated by Marco's unusual stories, but many also thought that he was a liar. They couldn't believe that what he told could be real. The disbelief was so great that the priest taking his confession on his deathbed in Venice (around the year 1324) asked Marco whether he was finally willing to confess his lies. Marco's answer was, "I did not tell half of what I really experienced, because I knew that the people wouldn't believe it anyway."

Something similar happens to people with NDEs. They are convinced that what they have seen on their travels is very real. Even though it seems out of this world, they know that it is more real than everyday life. And like Marco Polo, they know that many people won't be able to believe their stories.

This book would not have been there without the messages from NDErs. Their elevated knowledge comes at a cost. After their experiences, they find it extremely difficult to cope with our four-dimensional world again. On average, it takes them about seven years to find a kind of balance between their earthly life and their brush with heaven. Moreover, not only do the NDErs find it difficult, so do their loved ones. That is why I have asked what advice they have for people who are still struggling with their NDE, or who are still about to have their experience (see Chapter 10). It might be you!

CHAPTER 2

HEAVEN IS OUR BIRTHRIGHT

"I cannot describe what I have experienced. I am speechless. I can give no words to it. It is so sensational. Something new has been added to my thinking and to my being, to who I am. It is so spectacular. It is much more spectacular than any work of man and it is very well constructed..."

~(ROBERT) CHRISTOPHOR COPPES

This is the epilogue of my first book *Michael's Circle: Living with AIDS*, about friends and family supporting an AIDS patient during the last half year of his life. It is an anthology of quotes from NDErs.

Near-Death Experiences are extraordinary experiences.[1] Even mainstream science has admitted to that. There has been a lot of fine research and more is on its way. Hopefully it will bring further clarity into this matter. Regardless, those who have had these extraordinary experiences are stunned by them and are convinced that they are real. Most of them, especially those with a deep NDE, even believe that their experience is more real than their day-to-day life. What we have here on earth is a surrogate reality; it is merely a weak imprint of the reality they have experienced over there. They don't need proof. They know.

Those who have had an NDE believe with a firm conviction that the experience is absolutely true and because of the overwhelming beatifying character of the experience, they are convinced they have been on the other side, in heaven, or at least on its threshold. Interestingly, they also strongly feel that they originate from that environment and that they will eventually go back to it. Moreover, they feel that they belong there, that it is truly *home.*

When they talk about their life-changing experiences, they often get very emotional even years after the experiences, and they long to go back. They want to go home. It is a kind of homesickness. They completely lose their fear of death, because home is beyond death. On that other side, they have experienced unconditional love and complete acceptance of who they are. They say that everyone, in principle, is able to go there. The moment we are born, we acquire the right to return to this place. It is our birthright.

But what are these experiences? And how can we be sure that they are real? Before we take a closer look at some of the aspects of reported NDEs, we constantly have to keep in mind that NDErs have great difficulty in expressing what they have experienced. Their experiences are ineffable. They lack sufficient words or concepts to express what they have experienced. It is so completely new, so spectacular, and definitely not of this world, that they cannot put it into words. This applies to both the beautiful and positive experiences, as well as the terrifying and distressing ones. Unfortunately, these also exist (see Chapter 7).

Please read the quotes, appreciate them, and rejoice in them because they hold a beautiful promise for us all. However, at the same time, realize that the truth cannot be expressed properly due to the vastness and greatness of the real thing, and the lack of adequate earthly words and concepts.

Every NDE is unique

The term "Near-Death Experience" was coined by Raymond Moody, a medical doctor. He noticed that some of his patients seemed to have a vivid memory of the period during which they were clinically dead. These patients sometimes saw what doctors were doing, but they also talked with great happiness about encountering a blissful Light and deceased relatives. At that time, he was unaware that these experiences were not restricted to people who were nearly dead.

We now know that NDEs can happen to people in virtually any circumstance. There are stories of people who had their experience during an existential crisis, when they were meditating, or even when simply relaxing. I have even heard someone say that it happened in the middle of a conversation. It immediately put an end to the conversation because the person who had the NDE was completely flabbergasted by what he had experienced during some brief moments. Nevertheless, these cases are very rare. In most cases, an NDE occurs when people are in a critical medical situation. Of course, this includes life-threatening accidents. The reason seems to be that in these cases, the body is unable to hold the spirit any longer, and the spirit has the chance to "escape."

Not only do the causes of NDEs differ, but also the contents and the sequence in which the events take place. If we had to determine a prototype NDE, then it would start with an out-of-body experience in which, from a distance, the NDEr sees his body and the situation in which the body is (for example, the damaged car against the concrete wall or nurses and doctors running around frantically trying to keep the body alive). If there was pain, it disappears completely, leaving absolute peace and tranquility. Then there would be a tunnel and at the end of it one would see a pinpoint of light. The NDEr approaches it at a very high speed, and once there, one would find oneself in an unearthly and extremely beautiful and wonderfully light environment. There are magnificent trees, exquisite flowers with brilliant colors, and shining buildings. Beings of light, or perhaps even The Light itself would welcome you with unconditional love. At that moment, you would be shown your life review. Finally, there would be a type of boundary in the form of a river, a gate, or just a veil that you are not allowed to cross, or there would be someone telling you that it is better to go back.

The prototype rarely occurs. All NDEs are different. Some people only experience the first bit with the out-of-body experience, or the feeling of peace and tranquility. Other people immediately proceed to meeting beings of light. In many cases, there is no tunnel at all, and one NDEr had her life review before she traveled through a tunnel. Realize that the term "NDE" is used for extraordinary experiences in many different forms and intensities, and that for this reason, an unambiguous definition is not really possible. In addition, there seems to be a cultural aspect in NDEs.[2] During their experience, some people have spotted religious celebrities, but it is interesting to note, for instance, that Hindus don't generally see Maria or Jesus, while Christians don't generally see Mohammed or Krishna. In addition, Jesus does not always have the same appearance. In a panel during the 2005 IANDS[3] conference on NDEs, there were several people telling about their experience. They had all seen Jesus, and, astonishingly, they had different descriptions of him. He had black, brown, and even orange hair; brown eyes, dark eyes, or even blue eyes.

Apparently, the world NDErs visit is created entirely by their own consciousness, and for that reason, it is different for each human.[4] One might be led to think that NDEs are hallucinations, but though there is no solid evidence, there is plenty of reason to believe that this is not the case. This will be discussed further on. Therefore, there should be another explanation for the differences. Perhaps the images the NDErs see may be suited to their own individual situation, in order not to scare them, but to lovingly welcome them instead. Maybe for this reason NDErs are also welcomed by deceased relatives and friends, and occasionally even by their dogs. Or perhaps the images have been used to facilitate the memory once the NDEr returns from this inexplicable, heavenly environment. Remember, our words and concepts are absolutely inadequate for the NDErs to even remotely describe what they have seen and felt.

No limits

During their experiences, NDErs discover that they are not limited by anything. This applies to knowledge, observation, and place and time, to mention just a few. To non-NDErs, this sounds absurd, but then we have to remember that science has moved on and some scientists (some of whom are Nobel Prize winners) are considering theories in which time and place become relative notions.

NDErs say that their knowledge expands to such a high degree that they instantaneously get answers to all the questions they have. Their questions are even answered before they are posed: "I felt as if all the answers to all the questions I had ever wanted to ask, were answered simultaneously.

It wasn't like I knew any one specific answer. It was more like I just knew everything there was to know, ever. I also had the feeling that as I received this knowledge from the beings of light, I in turn gave to them all the unique experiences that I had accumulated from my time alive on earth. They gave me what they had, and I gave them what I had to contribute. It was very pleasing to do this exchange. I felt completely free and content."[5]

It is impossible to take all that knowledge back to earth again. It is simply too much for our brains to process and to contain. One NDEr even said that she regularly had to rest her brain because she had received too much information. This information comes from an environment that is completely different from what we have been experiencing during our lifetime in our four-dimensional world.

This knowledge comes to the NDEr in the form of awareness. It is awareness without sensation. This is especially clear in the cases of blind NDErs.[6] One person who was born blind said that he, of course, had no idea if the images he saw during his experience were visual. He described it as follows: "…a tactual sense, like I could really feel with the fingers of my mind. But I did not remember actually touching the snow. The only thing I can really state about those images was that they came to me in an awareness and that I was aware of those images in a way I did not really understand."[7]

Another NDEr said that through this awareness he knew everything. "I knew every thought and every idea that every person had, ever had, or would ever have. These were like voices (though there was no sound, so how could they be voices) over-heard in a crowded restaurant, but I could distinctly hear and follow each conversation all at once without any one distract-ing me from another."[8]

While the nurses were considering what to do, an NDEr described herself as gliding through the operating room as if she was sitting on a fluffed up eiderdown cloud. She floated around the lamp and along the clock, which seemed to be huge from so near by. Then she saw a doctor rushing through the corridors of the hospital; she could see him even though he was several corridors away. She could actually look through walls! In addition, she realized that her glasses (-10.5) were still next to her bed; normally, without them, she has blurred vision.

Other NDErs also notice that there is something strange going on with how they perceive things. Some claim that they can see objects from all sides, as if they have thousands of eyes. They can look at them simultaneously from every angle imaginable. Nothing is impossible.

During an NDE, place is no limitation either. In many cases, NDErs can leave the place where their body is and travel without any effort, for instance, through cities or to their homes. Some even say they have traveled through the universe and have seen far away galaxies. One person said that he was "at the center of all places, at once, outside the known universe (or our understanding of it) and encompassing the entire universe."[9]

Like place, time is no limitation either. Time in NDEs is totally different from how we have learned to understand time on earth. NDErs have great difficulty in explaining this. They are certain about time having no limitations. Some quotes that illustrate this include:

✧ "Time doesn't exist."

✧ "I was hanging between eternity and 'normal' time."

✧ "All time exists at once."[10]

✧ "It was not in time, it was in between time."[11]

✧ "Everything is now. The past, the present, and the future are the same. They blend."

✧ "In this other place there is no linear time as we know it. Everything is experienced in the same moment."

✧ "Seeing history and the future can be compared with sitting in an airplane when you are able to see two different cities at the same time."[12]

✧ "There was no time in this place. Every moment of history and the present and the future were unfolded before me as one monumental event starting with the creation of the universe and ending—well that has since been blocked from me in such a way that it hurts to try to remember."[13]

Unconditional love

By far, the most important aspect of NDEs is love. The love they experience in their NDE is completely overwhelming and it thoroughly changes them after their experience. This is especially true when they meet The Light. Like everything else in an NDE, The Light is something NDErs find very difficult to describe. It communicates as if it is some kind of intelligent being, but then it is not really a being, but a radiant bright light that doesn't hurt your senses. It radiates an incredible amount of love. The Light's love is incomprehensible; its love is many times stronger and more intense than the love someone feels for their children. It surpasses everything. The Light is supreme love.

Some go to great lengths to express this in words. "When I would add all the love I had received throughout my life together, it would still be less than 1 percent of what I felt there."

And in a very graphic way, "About the best way to describe it is to take the best steak, the best lobster, the most spectacular view, the best booze, and the most exquisite sex with the most exquisite partner. In other words, take the best you have ever felt, done, been, however, any way, any how and take them all and throw them at you at once and it is just a small fraction of how delicious the feeling is."[14]

A very important aspect of The Light that is consistently stressed is that its love is unconditional. Try to realize what unconditional love actually means. It is love that is present without any preconditions. It is free to have and you don't need to do anything in particular to get it. There is no dress code: You don't have to be dressed in black or orange or any other color; there is no need for scarves or other frills. You don't need to cut your hair in a particular style. You can be bald, or have curls along the side. You can have a beard or not. You don't have to refrain from eating particular foods; there are no dietary restrictions. Shrimp is acceptable, as is pork or beef, and it is not a taboo should you choose to restrict yourself to eating only vegetables. There is no obligation to pray five times in a specific direction, you don't necessarily have to pray at all. This unconditional love is not withheld, even when you admit having caused harm to others or admit having done terrible things. There are simply no conditions to receiving this unconditional love of The Light.

You just have to be who you are; being who you are is good enough. You don't have to efface yourself. Quoting an NDEr as to what The Light had said to her, "Also with you I am well pleased." This is truly unconditional.

Life review

During their NDEs, some people have a life review, and this often occurs in the presence of The Light. A life review comes in many forms. Some see their life as a film in fast-forward mode. Some see flashes or pictures. Some feel that these are memories of events. The overall feeling is described as "this is you." The smallest details are perfectly clear. For instance, one NDEr vividly remembers the first moment of his life review, when the nurse wrapped the newborn in a cloth, saying, "Oh he has such lovely little ears!" Later, when he asked his mother about this, she was utterly surprised. "How did you know?"

In any case, the life review is a refresher. We get to remember the place we have in the grand universal scheme and the task which we have had on earth or, rather, which we still have.

After all, people with NDEs, whose testimonies were reported, have all returned to continue their life.

The life review also refreshes our memory in another way. It enables us to be conscious of potentially all events of our life and of the effect they have had on others. This consciousness comes in a very interesting way. We get to remember these events, not only as ourselves, but also as if we were the other people involved. We can see our own life from our own point of view, but also from the viewpoint of everyone else. For instance, we will feel the happiness of the people we did something nice for. We will feel their happiness as if we were them. Conversely, this also happens when we have harmed other people. We will feel their pain, as if we have harmed ourselves.

One woman once shared her candy with a school friend. It was just after the World War II in the Netherlands and candy back then was a rare luxury. During her life review, she felt the gratitude and happiness of her friend. She felt how thrilled her friend was to be considered worthy enough to receive that candy. The feeling of extreme happiness didn't stop with the friend, but she was surprised to notice it was extended to the mother of the friend as well. To her full amazement, she felt that the positive effect didn't stop there, either. In a very strange way, she felt that her kind gesture rippled further, to places she could not have imagined before. It had a great effect on the world because it increased the total energy in it.

However, this NDEr also found out that a negative act makes the energy of the world shrink. Another one of her school friends was suffering from lice and asked her for help.

She helped by offering to kill a few. The pitiful thing was that she didn't do it quietly. Instead, she made a big fuss out of it. By talking out loud about the lice, she exposed her friend.

During her life review, she could feel the extent of her friend's embarrassment. She could feel the pain and suffering from this humiliation, as if she was actually the friend herself. But worse than this painful feeling, was the feeling that she had failed in seizing the opportunity to add energy to the world.

She had the chance to bring love and warmth, but she didn't make the most of it. From her life review she understood that the goal, dead lice, was not important at all. Instead, the way she went about achieving this goal was important. She had chosen to make a great commotion, but she could also have chosen to work in silence. In that case, in addition to the dead lice there would have been something else: She would have comforted her friend and given her the feeling that she is appreciated, even with the little monsters crawling through her hair. Wasting that wonderful opportunity felt like an awful shame.

The whole event seemed not to be a matter of wrong or right, but a matter of becoming thoroughly conscious of what had happened. She could reach this high level of consciousness because she was able to feel a very deep empathy, also toward herself. There was no punishment, although maybe the feeling of wasting a good opportunity was in itself a sort of punishment. But the word punishment still isn't right; it is more something of a very deep sorrow, which was most hurtful.

There is something remarkable about The Light. The Light does not call us to account, which is peculiar when you imagine how the setting is. During our life review, we see all the facts and feelings in and around our life as it passes by, even the secret ones, the ones we try to hide from others. All the pain and grief we inflicted is indisputably displayed in unmistakable terms and in all intensity and detail. In a way, we are defenseless: we cannot hide from the review and we cannot stop it. The truth is revealed, and both we and The Light see it. We can only feel deeply ashamed for all our unkind actions. Despite all that, The Light does not call us to account. It does not change a bit. It remains totally loving. It remains full of understanding and full of forgiveness, and in spite of all our shortcomings, It continues to accept us unconditionally.

In the presence of this completely perfect and unconditional love that surrounds us warmly, something happens within ourselves. We feel our own shortcomings. We assess all our actions and thoughts, and we do all that by ourselves. There aren't any bibles produced, no Koran is opened, no Bhagavad Gita, no lists of do's and don'ts. No rabbi comes along; no priest, imam, Brahmin, or lama is consulted. We literally assess ourselves in the light of the overwhelming love in which we are present at that moment, while being endowed with all knowledge of everything that was, is, and shall be.

Some people say that a kind of discussion is started about their life, though not in words, but in thoughts. Sometimes the discussion is conducted with The Light, and sometimes with other beings that they encounter there. The discussion, however, never has an accusing tone. Nobody is aggressive, and nobody is stamping his or her feet telling us how wrong we were. It is rather like being asked questions to make us more conscious of the things we did. Why did you do that? What were you thinking when you said this? What ulterior motive were you concealing from the others? And why? If anyone is doing the judging, then it is us. We do the judging ourselves.

Some NDErs have even noticed that when they were too harsh in their own judgment, The Light assured them not to be. It seems to be sufficient to be conscious of what happened in our lives, and to understand how deep or shallow our feelings of love were.

We are experiencing what we did to others as if it is done to us, because we feel the complete interconnectedness with those others. In addition, we are judging ourselves in the process. I find these two special effects extremely remarkable. Firstly, because many NDErs say that these two together are the most powerful motivators to alter their lives. They really enhance consciousness about one's own life. Secondly, these two effects are something a normal person could not have thought of. This is so extraordinary, and in a way, so unearthly, that it is actually an innovation in our thinking of a final judgment after we die. And this is one of the things that convince me that NDEs truly give us a first glimpse of heaven.

Stairway to heaven

After their experiences, the NDErs are never the same any-more. Something fundamental has changed. More will be discussed about this (see Chapter 10), but here we have to recognize that the experience has created an opening, which will never completely close again. The "stairway to heaven" is still there.

It is very common for NDErs to become rather sensitive. They know things, or they have abilities that are out of the ordinary, and that they didn't have before. For instance, some are able to detect the emotions of others. They feel their pain or sorrow. One NDEr told me that he was able to sense everything about others after he touched them. Some could feel when people were not telling the truth. Many NDErs develop a paranormal sensitivity, which enables some to correctly predict the future. For instance, one NDEr always knew exactly whether she had to run in order to catch the next bus or could just leisurely walk to the bus stop. Of course there was a time-table, but it was useless since the buses were usually caught up in traffic.

Another example is from an NDEr who was visiting his cousin and his wife in Yakima, Washington, in May of 1979. All three went on a tour through the state. At one point, they drove along Mount St. Helens. They made some jokes about how it would be if the volcano would start working, but the wife of the cousin said that the volcano had been silent for hundreds of years. The NDEr suddenly said, "Next year it will errupt. You'll think of me then." Exactly a year later, the volcano exploded.

Some NDErs still have the ability to leave their body. I spoke to an elderly woman, Diana, who told me that she sometimes could still travel around and go to places she could not afford to go. This doesn't happen in the physical way; it happens in a manner unknown to her, in a spiritual sort of way. She has no control over this. She cannot decide, for instance, that on Monday afternoon she is going to visit India. She cannot evoke these kinds of experiences, but she can feel them coming. And fortunately, it doesn't happen when she is at the grocery store.

On one occasion, she spent a whole day in the savannah in Africa, watching the sun rise above the horizon and set again in the evening. In the meantime, she was able to feel the environment, the animals, and the vegetation. She hovered around and felt the energy of the plants and animals that she came across. What impressed her most were the paws of the lions she saw. She came very close; she was inches away, and it was as if the lions could feel her presence. They looked up, sniffed in the air, looked in her direction, sniffed again, but finally settled peacefully. The movement of one lioness made sand roll off her back. Diana noticed it, because she could hear it clearly. It rumbled loudly over the lion's hair, as if in slow motion. Apparently her senses were much heightened.

In the same way, Diana had been present when a woman from a homecare service was robbed in a streetcar. Diana saw it happen, but, of course, could not prevent it. The woman was heading to attend to Diana. Despite the robbery, she didn't want to keep Diana waiting and decided to go to the police afterward. When she arrived, Diana said, "What are you doing here? You have to go to the police now!" The woman from homecare was utterly shocked that Diana knew, and left immediately.

Some NDErs have the ability to heal others or themselves. One NDEr had three broken ribs, and bruised kidneys, spleen, and liver.[15] He was bleeding internally and the doctors didn't know exactly where. He said he was going to consciously heal himself. He said he could feel what was wrong with his body. "I could redirect blood flow and nutrients to areas that needed it and away from areas that were bleeding. I could will my flesh and bones to grow back together. When I had a CT scan, the technicians ran another because the readings were so strange. There was no brain damage whatsoever, which was considered impossible given the extent of my injuries and how long my brain had been without oxygen while I was clinically dead."

He woke up in the middle of the night and realized that his doctor was sitting in a chair in his room. "I told him he could go tend to someone else if he needed, that I was going to be fine. He said, 'I know, but what's happening to you is unbelievable. You should be dead. I can't turn my back on a miracle. God is allowing me the opportunity to witness this and I just can't walk away.' I later found out that his daughter had been in a car accident and had similar injuries. He had been questioning God and he thought what was happening to me before his eyes was God's answer that He was still here."

Veridical observations

During the period NDErs have left their bodies, some of them make observations that could be verified later. There are many of these so called stories of veridical out-of-body perceptions, but only a few have been sufficiently well-documented. The reason for this low score is, of course, that these observations always occur unannounced. Even though some of these well-documented veridical perceptions are very convincing, they are always subject to skepticism by people who clutch on to the pure material interpretation of the functioning of the brain. According to them, consciousness cannot exist without the brain; it is the product of the brain. They do everything in their power to demonstrate the incorrectness of the documented perception, and even resort to ridiculing the involved doctors, nurses, and scientists. Convinced materialistic skeptics can be compared to religious fundamentalists; their rigid views make it very difficult to discuss things with them.

It should be mentioned that there have been several clinical studies that have tried to prove the existence of out-of-body experiences. However, these studies haven't been able to come up with one objective case of veridical perception. At the moment, extensive research is being conducted involving 25 medical centers throughout the world. The study focuses on awareness during resuscitation, and is known by the acronym AWARE (AWAreness during REsuscitation). Although many NDErs have their doubts about the protocol, this research will perhaps come up with some strong evidence. Until then we have to rely on the random, but-well documented cases. I will mention three.

The tennis shoe[16]

A patient floated out of her body toward a ledge outside the hospital. There she saw a tennis shoe, which had some detailed characteristics. Because she was brought into the hospital that particular evening, she could not have known about the ledge, let alone where the tennis shoe was. The shoe was indeed found there.

The man with dentures[17]

This case is mentioned in the research by the cardiologist Pim van Lommel published in the *Lancet,* a highly rated medical journal. A man was found in a Dutch meadow suffering a massive heart attack. During the ambulance ride, several resuscitation attempts were made. In the hospital, the three nurses who took over the resuscitation noticed that the patient didn't have blood circulation, nor did he have ventilation in the lungs. Moreover, he had no noticeable consciousness, his features were gray and he seemed to already have postmortem lividity.

One of the nurses tried to intubate the patient to give artificial respiration, but found out that the patient had a set of false teeth. He removed the dentures, and put them in a wooden drawer in a crash cart. It was in 1979, and at that time, crash carts were not as common as they are now. This particular cart was made out of an ordinary kitchen cart. Therefore, it was primitive but unique. The resuscitation took about an hour, which is quite long, but eventually was successful. The nurse went home and had a week-long vacation.

When he came back from his vacation, his schedule was to attend to patients, amongst which was the patient he had helped resuscitate. Even though the patient had been in a coma for a week, he immediately recognized the nurse. To the amazement of the nurse, he was able to tell him where he had put his dentures. He said he had been hovering close to the ceiling, and had seen everything that happened, including the whole procedure. He could describe the room, even the recessed sink, which he could not have seen from where he was lying in bed. He also described the crash cart, where they finally found his dentures.

Operation standstill[18]

Finally, a well-documented, well-known case of a young woman with swelling in one of the main blood vessels in her brain was featured on the BBC as a documentary. The swelling was to be surgically removed. This particular swelling can be pictured like a bubble on the side of a defective car tire. Under extreme medical conditions, she underwent a daring new surgical procedure known as hypothermic cardiac arrest. The nickname of this operation, standstill, is clearer than the medical term and illustrates exactly what the procedure does.

She was cooled to a temperature of 60 degrees Fahrenheit (about 15 degrees Celsius), her breathing and heartbeat were stopped, her brain waves flattened to a complete stop, and all blood was removed from her head. All of this was done to reduce the size of the swelling, as if the air were being taken out of a defective tire. In this manner, the deflated bubble could easily be incised and removed. Then everything was switched on again, and the body returned to the normal temperature.

During the whole surgery, which lasted about an hour and 25 minutes, she was very carefully monitored. While her eyes were closed and taped, and her ears were plugged, she experienced that she was pulled out of the top of her head. She later told that there was this sound that had pulled her out. It was "a frequency that you go on," as if it was a road. That was the start of a very deep NDE in which she accurately saw details of the surgical procedures and instruments. As if she was sitting on the surgeon's shoulder, she said, she had a brighter, more focused and clearer vision of everything that was happening. She had expected that the nurses would have shaved all her hair off for the operation, but they had not done so.

Before entering the operating room, she could not have seen the instruments that were going to be used, because the instruments were kept in their packaging for hygienic reasons. Nevertheless, she would later give a good description of the bone saw. She said that it was like an electric toothbrush and that it had interchangeable blades.

Her ears were plugged with speakers that emitted 100-decibel clicks. This was done to stimulate brain activity (hearing) which, if there was brain activity, would show up on the electrocardiogram. Despite the plugging of her ears and the loud clicks they sent into them, she overheard the conversation between the surgeon and the nurse about how her veins were too small. She also described the bone saw's sound as being high-pitched and how suddenly "it went *brrrrrrrr.*"

Apart from having no heartbeat, blood pressure, or respiration, her brain waves also flattened and finally the brain totally shut down. Remember, all of this was monitored very carefully. She was clinically dead for more than an hour. After her blood was drained from her body "like oil from a car" (she said), she was pulled away from the scene. It was not against her will, she said later, but it was of her own accord. Then she went through the tunnel where she heard her grandmother calling her. Subsequently, she saw The Light, and finally she saw many other deceased people in this Light, amongst them, her grandmother. Even though all the spirits were friendly, they would not permit her to go any further. She had to go back and, fortunately, that was also what she desired for herself, because she wanted to look after her children. She was told that if she would go any further into The Light, returning would no longer be possible. "Something would happen to me physically. They would be unable to put this ME back into the body ME, like I had gone too far and they couldn't reconnect. So they wouldn't let me go anywhere or do anything."

The getting back part is interesting, too. Her uncle guided her back through the tunnel. At the end, she saw "the thing, my body." She didn't want to get back into it. Her uncle gently pushed her into that thing and it felt "like diving into a pool of ice water."

The interesting aspect of this case is that the whole procedure was so well documented, especially during the time she had been clinically dead. This medical account could then be compared with the account of the patient. From this, it became clear that, during her cardiac arrest, she had had a coherent perception of all that took place in the operating room. Moreover, while there was no brain activity, she was perfectly conscious, and she experienced other things that she could remember in a coherent way. This medical case seems to provide very strong proof of consciousness being separated from the body, while existing by itself.

Could there be more dimensions?

Until now, in this chapter, we have seen that in NDEs, there are no physical or time limits, a vast and unconditional love is there for everyone, an infinite knowledge is freely available to tap into, and life reviews are not only very detailed, but also presented in such a way that one can feel exactly what others have felt. I have been thinking of how to explain all of this, and the only thing I can come up with is that there are most likely more dimensions than we know of. Currently we think there are four. There are the three space dimensions, plus time. And time comes in just one form: linear. We can only go forward in the present; we cannot go back into history, or advance quickly enough to arrive in the future. It will always be the present. However, the existence of five or even more dimensions does not seem to be unthinkable anymore.

It started with Einstein (and his general theory of relativity), who theorized that time is not as absolute as experienced in our daily life. Afterward, quantum mechanics came with its "uncertainty principle," which, in fact, ended the scientific belief in an absolute objective certainty. Currently, there are scientists, some of whom are Nobel Prize winners, working on unifying theories, called string theories. These theories seem to be consistent only if space-time has more dimensions (10 or even 26 dimensions were mentioned), instead of the usual four. [19]

Even if there is only one extra dimension, it would be something we will never be able to understand or describe with our current concepts. Just imagine how it would be if people lived in a world with only three dimensions, and then some of them were given the once-in-a-lifetime chance to get a glimpse of a four-dimensional world (our current world).[20] A three-dimensional world would be a world where flat creatures live (two dimensions) who have knowledge of time (the third dimension). If there were things resembling trees, they would be completely different from our trees because they would be flat. Flat people can walk around a flat tree but, by definition, can never climb it. They wouldn't even know the concept of climbing, because height does not exist in their flat world.

Should we step on to this flat world and walk around it, flat people would only see where we put our feet. For them, something would suddenly appear, then disappear again, and then suddenly emerge once more a little further on. They would have no idea what it is and would never be able to describe exactly what it is. They would perhaps call it a ghost that would appear and disappear, or maybe a random moving apparition. In any case, they would have no idea whatsoever about the whole body that is attached to that moving apparition.

Imagine what would happen if one of them experienced our four-dimensional world for a brief moment. He would be completely bewildered, and upon returning to his flat world, would never be able to describe to his fellow flat people what he had seen. How could he ever express that these moving apparitions are just a minor part, or even just an imprint, of a whole body that is attached to it? He would say incomprehensible and cryptic things to his brothers and sisters, such as, "The other world is more real, you have more possibilities, you can move more freely, you can see in different directions at the same time and even though we cannot see it, that world is all around us."

If you are an NDEr, or if you have spoken to an NDEr about his or her experience, then you recognize these "incomprehensible and cryptic" remarks. Now think of the communication between the two worlds. The flat people wouldn't be able to communicate with us, because they don't know how we perceive things. They could make forms, which we could read, but how would they know that we can see them from above?

As for us, how could we communicate with them when they can't hear sound waves, or see light waves, which are three-dimensional? The only thing we can do is appear and disappear again, but that would only startle the flat people.

This little mind experiment is presented to demonstrate that when there are essential differences between two worlds, it is very difficult for the presence of a meaningful interaction between the two. This might be the reason why it seems impossible to prove that there is a much greater world around us, and that NDEs are the first phase of our entry into this world.

Scientific research

The study of NDEs began with the pioneering work of doctors such as Elisabeth Kübler-Ross and Raymond Moody.[21] Elisabeth Kübler-Ross was a Swiss woman who emigrated after the World War II to the United States, where she was affected by the stories of her terminally ill patients. She created a list of the five stages which they generally pass through: denial, anger, bargaining, depression, and acceptance. [22] Moody was the first person to use the term "Near-Death Experience." He studied a large number of NDEs amongst his patients and described many common characteristics.

The first series of research, which started with Kübler-Ross and Moody was retrospective and anecdotal. There was no systematic approach to find NDErs. Researchers came into contact with them accidentally, which could easily be many years after their experience. According to mainstream science, this is not the right method to carry out research.

This changed in 2001, when a group of scientists led by the Dutch cardiologist Pim van Lommel published the results of the first prospective study in the *Lancet*. This is a highly respected international medical journal. [23] This study was carried out in 10 different Dutch hospitals during a 13-year period. It was designed according to accepted scientific standards, because a systematic approach was followed to find NDErs: Each patient who had a cardiac arrest (this is an objective critical medical situation), and who was successfully resuscitated in the coronary care units of the participating hospitals were included in the database. Shortly after recovery from their cardiac arrest, each one was asked whether they had a recollection of the period during which they had been unconscious. By following this strict rule, the researchers wanted to eliminate any subjective judgment as to whether or not to include a patient in the research. This so-called prospective procedure was aimed at creating an objective pool of people who had an NDE, and compare them with people from the same database that did not have an NDE. The differences could give an indication of what causes NDEs.

However, no differences were found between the group of people with an NDE and the group without. For instance, individuals in both groups were suffering from an insufficient supply of oxygen to the brain. Therefore, a lack of oxygen could finally be excluded as a cause (critics had always cited it as the number one cause for NDEs). Individuals in both groups were in the process of dying, and should have experienced similar physiological changes in the brain. For that reason, the possible creation of certain hallucinatory chemicals by dying brain cells could also be excluded as a cause. In this way, many more factors were excluded. Nevertheless, the real cause has yet to be established, but NDErs have no doubts: They are absolutely certain they have had a glimpse of the invisible part of universe.

There have been several other comparable prospective studies, but they are either based on smaller samples[24] or the protocol for the study was less extensive.[25] Nevertheless, the results are more or less similar to those of the Dutch study.

Yet, another kind of prospective research was carried out in the moments just after NDErs had left their body. These are interesting moments, because in most cases, NDErs start floating just below the ceiling of an operating room where they can observe, to their own utter amazement, how the doctors and nurses are trying to rescue them. The test consists of putting hidden visual targets in the operating room, which, hopefully, the NDErs would see during their experience and would report after their resuscitation. This veridical NDE research is limited to just five studies and had minimal or no findings.[26] Experiencers themselves are quite skeptical about this kind of research. They say that the NDE is so bewildering that they have other things on their minds than spotting hidden visual targets on a shelf or cupboard.

Because of the disappointing results in these studies, a new, more comprehensive research (the previously mentioned

AWARE study) was designed and started in 2008. It is a three-year exploration of the biology behind out-of-body experiences. It involves 25 major medical centers across Europe, Canada and the United States where some 1,500 survivors of cardiac arrest will be examined.

Chapter 3

The Unity Universe

"This Light was 'home.' It was more home than I had experienced anywhere or anytime in my life. This Light was peace, it was equality for everyone, it was security, it was recognition. And I was part of it. I was completely one in and with that Light. I was allowed to be there."

~Marga van Lennep-Kernkamp

Marga had her NDE a day after she gave birth to her daughter. She had lost a lot of blood and her body didn't accept the necessary blood transfusion.[1]

Take a look at some of the things NDErs have said about their experiences and concentrate on the reoccurring themes. After people leave their bodies, they gain a tremendous awareness. It is as if they become awareness itself and, through this awareness, they can sense everything there is to sense. There is no physical limitation. For instance, they don't need glasses or even eyes to see. They can look at objects from many different angles at the same time. Walls are no obstacles; with this specific kind of awareness, they can look through them. And there are no boundaries for going places; they can just move through concrete if they choose. They can go wherever they want to go, so physical place is no limitation.

On top of that, time is no limitation, either. It doesn't exist, or rather, it exists all at once. They can see the future and the past. It is all there at the same time: the past, the present, and the future. They are the same. They blend.

All knowledge becomes theirs. It is all freely accessible. They are able to know everything they want to know. Every thought and every idea that every person has ever had or will ever have is open and available to them.

And finally, the energy that is felt is enormous. It surpasses everything. Its greatness is incomprehensible, and it seems to be made from love. Love constitutes this unlimited vastness and infinite power. This power *is love*. And this love *is unconditional*. While we are in this Light, we are able to see every tiny detail of our life, because every little bit is still there. The most striking thing of all is that we are able to access it and feel what others around us have felt, and what our actions have triggered in them. We feel it as if we are them, as if these feelings are ours. A more direct feeling of what we did to others is not possible. It shows that, in fact, there is no real division between us and others. There is a perfect interconnection.

All of this implies unity. Consequently, we are part of one big whole. We are part of a unity universe.

Everyone carries The Light

One of the most astonishing things NDErs consistently say is that everyone and everything is interconnected through The Light. Or, similarly, we are interconnected through love. Everyone is part of The Light. Someone said that each human can be likened to a grain of sand on a wide beach, while The Light is the whole beach.[2] Also someone said that we are all children of God, and therefore, we all are little Gods, too. We just have to remember our divinity.[3] Note that this is one of the essences of Hinduism: Everyone has a God in him or her. You will not find that in any of the other major religions.

The Light is not something outside of us. We all carry it within. It is in everything—in animals, trees, flowers, and even in stone and steel. It flows through us.[4] It wants to flow and breathe through us. And this flow or presence of The Light in all of us makes NDErs say that everyone belongs to one great whole. We are one, and in this oneness we, in fact, are perfect.

One NDEr said, "The whole was the collective knowledge of all. I understood there was no individual, just one, yet each experience was individual making up the whole. This concept of ONE is so foreign to any description I can give, there seems to be no way of describing it. Many being one and one being many, both existing simultaneously in the same time and space. The collective experiences are omniscient knowledge. Everything that has been spoken, heard, and experienced. These colored drops contained each experience down to the memory of every cell division, every thought. All experiences were known at once by the collective consciousness that was the stream. Any experience could be known as if it were a first person experience happening at the time it happened originally. I was shown a long line of experiences in other realms of realities and on other worlds. It was some time later I realized it was my past lives review of all existences of which I had been part."[5]

Another said that with the wonderful Light, there was also an incredible feeling of love and peace. She could feel this wonderful love and peace through and through. It was a unique and complete feeling, and nothing that she knew on earth could compare with it. That love, she said, is what connects us with each other, and with everything there is.

The consequence of all of us being interconnected in this unity universe is that we are connected to, for instance, the president of the United States, but also to the homeless person in the street. This may be shocking to some of us, but it shouldn't be. On the contrary, it should make us happy, because if we were all conscious of our interconnection, we would be living in a much better world. Actually, NDErs do realize this and their experience inspires them to respect everyone.

The interconnectedness also means that our world is not separated from that other world. It is part of it. It belongs to it. It is just as important as that heavenly environment that NDErs speak of. Actually, there is no division. Heaven, or however we choose to refer to it, is very close. It is all around us. And to quote the Quran on this, Allah/God says in his majestic plural, "We are nearer to man than his jugular vein."[6]

The fundamental interconnectedness was also felt by a little 4-year-old. It happened during World War II in the former Dutch colony of what is now Indonesia. A few years ago, she wrote a magnificent book about her life.[7]

The Japanese had overrun the colony, and incarcerated the Dutch in concentration camps. The treatment was terrible, absolutely inhumane. For instance, people were forced to be present at the roll call. For hours, they had to stand in the burning sun. It didn't matter whether someone was ill; everyone had to stand there. Tienke was small and frail. She was undernourished, and was suffering from cholera. All of a sudden, she had her first NDE and one of the things she heard was, "There is no friend and enemy; it is a silly game of adults; it is not the Truth."

This event had a great impact on her life. Suddenly, she had an overview of the situation she was in, and, as small as she was, she received the knowledge to see that the division between the suppressors and the suppressed was artificial. It wasn't necessary and it didn't have to be so. She understood that the people who terrified others were basically equal to the people who they terrified. She understood this, because she became fully aware that the divine power doesn't make a division between friend and enemy. There is no division between them and us. We make that division ourselves. We put blinders on ourselves.[8]

Despite this revealing experience, she was still subject to the regime of terror in the concentration camp. It didn't stop just because she had her experience. It didn't even stop after the Japanese lost the war and withdrew, which freed her, at last, to go back to Holland with her parents. Like any other person who had lived in a concentration camp, she had to learn later on in her life, to cope with her horrendous experiences. Despite her revealing NDE, it took a lot of effort.

Duality

Even though we are all *one* and we all belong to the unity universe, the power of this Light also allows separation. Separation is a major phenomenon in our four-dimensional world. Our world seems specifically designed for separation. From the moment we are born, we learn to perceive two things: ourselves and the rest of the world. At first, the baby identifies itself with its parents and has no ego, but it soon finds out that it is a dual world. It is me and them. Of course, the senses perform wonders to discover this distinction. They are an excellent help in completing that perception of duality. For instance, a child touching a red hot kettle on the stove discovers that no one else is hurt but him- or herself.

The discoveries don't stop there. We discover that we are different from others, that we are individuals, and that each individual has its own personality. The individual can therefore say: I need food, I need something to drink, don't hurt me, I need shelter, I need this job. And after a lot of development, we find out that we have grown an ego: *I don't only need this job, I want it, I want a fancy car that goes with it, I want a Rolls Royce, don't you dare leave me, I hate you, I love you, I need you,* and so on.

This ego is the final result of the ultimate structure in which our consciousness lives—our body. This ultimate structure determines the boundaries of our consciousness. Or at least, for most people including me, it feels that way. NDErs, who have had the opportunity to leave their body, have discovered that this artificial limitation is not real. They have felt that they are part of something so much bigger, and that it has always been that way. They continue to have that conviction, even after returning to their body. They know that their body restricts their view, and for that reason, they call it a prison, a shell, or a wet suit that feels just a tiny bit too small.

They find out that the body is a structure they have to learn to live and cope with. At the same time, they realize that it is only one of many structures they are confronted with during their life. There are many more, and they can be found anywhere. These are not only the physical structures, but also those we create with our mind: parental authority, the police, regulators, supervisors, the state, the church, religions, and, of course, money. Structures and constructs are something we apparently need. They can be beneficial to us, and help us in life, but we have to recognize that sometimes they can turn against us by being too restrictive or even flawed and terribly harmful. For instance, at one time, we thought of witches and we started to believe that they exist. Then, for many centuries, we hunted them and we have even burned them—or rather—we burned innocent men and women whom we thought were witches.

The point is, that our protracted and painful upbringing in this dual world restricts our view. For one thing, it has obscured our view on the unity universe. We are so much focused on our body and other material structures, and on our mental constructs, that we even started to doubt the existence of the invisible part of the unity universe.

NDErs visited this part of the unity universe and felt its existence. It convinced them that it is there. They know what it is to float freely, to feel free, and to feel a bond with everything else. Some say that what we perceive of ourselves on earth is but a small part of what we really are. According to one NDEr: "You are a big body of light, but not all of that light is in your earthly body. The biggest part is elsewhere. When you die, you will merge again and feel whole."

Having part of this huge body of light return to the restricted four-dimensional world is a painful process, many

NDErs say. Returning back to their body brings them back in firmer and more solid structures. An NDEr said, "That was so painful, both mentally and physically. While going lower and lower, the love left me and was replaced by more structures, until, with a *bang!*, I fell in my body again. And that, of course, is a solid structure."[9]

Longing to go back

After their return, they long to go back to that world of freedom, where there is a place for them, where they only have to be, where there is love, peace, tranquility, equality, recognition, and security; that world without all those imposing structures, boundaries, and many do's and don'ts. That beneficial free feeling NDErs experienced makes them intensely resent limiting and oppressing structures.

One of the constructs that man created, and NDErs usually have problems with, is time. It is something rigid, something with a distinct touch of solidity. NDErs often have problems with its inflexibility. Many of them have the habit of arriving late at appointments or missing deadlines. They also often dislike working in fixed schedules. This aversion to time sometimes even materializes. Watches and clocks may stop keeping time, and one NDEr assured me that there is no reason for her to wear a watch, because it always breaks down. Moreover, the clocks in her house strike wrong and new clock batteries last for just one week. Only the radio-alarm works properly because it is connected to the main supply. Nevertheless, even without clocks, she arrives for her appointments more or less on time.

Not being able to cope with time is just one of the problems NDErs have with constructs. Many more could be mentioned. One NDEr said, "Foreigners? There are no foreigners; there are no illegal people. How can people be illegal? No one is more than another. God wants the best for us, more than we can ever dare to dream of. But He wants the best for all of us. He doesn't draw boundaries. God is also freedom. We pose restrictions on ourselves. We make prisons in our own head. We even allow others to make prisons in our own head by accepting the restrictions they pose upon us."

And another one said, "An oak tree may be an oak tree in all its aspects. There are no restrictions. Likewise, every person should be himself in all his aspects. It is wrong not to acknowledge the value and authenticity of someone else by imposing restrictions on him. Structures and constructs are restrictive. The mind is restricted too often. That is terrible. The mind should be free."

With respect to religions and the related structures NDErs sometimes seem to have some especially hard feelings:

✧ "I used to be a very religious Catholic, and I believed in the official doctrine. But that is over now! Everything is lied about. They only do it for their own profit. Religions scare people. No matter which religion, they all do it. The only good thing about a church is that people are together."

✧ "The Church is an earthly organization, eager for power."

✧ "I am sick of the Church as an institution; God is too limited by the Church, and misinterpreted. I'd like to speak of God as I experience God: as a healing energy and a loving Mind."[10]

✧ "Religious instruction was awful. They were talking about mortal sins and daily sins, and I told them they were dead wrong. The nun sent me out of the classroom!"

✧ "Religions should be based on love, but they aren't."

✧ "Every religion is okay; everyone is free to choose one. It is absolutely wrong of a religion when it advocates aggression. That is not religion. That cannot be right. People who believe that religions can resort to aggression have lost their minds. Repaying evil with evil doesn't work. Love works."

✧ "The key is not in one religion alone; it is in all together. God is The Light, and what we see are the colors of the rainbow. Yet, it is divided light; all the colors together are one again."

✧ "Religions are important, but should not be coercive."

✧ "Religions should build bridges to The Light."

✧ "Every religion has the essential value to make this life livable."

During his experience, one NDEr asked point-blank which religion is the best.[11] The answer was as short as it was clear: "The religion that brings you closest to God." From that answer, it is also clear that it does not matter which religion you believe in. "The purpose of religion is to have a personal relationship with God. Religion is only a means to find God. Religion is not a destination.... God is far greater than any religion."[12] This NDEr also gives us a warning. He says that God abhors it when people use religion for their own purposes or to demean other people. That is one of the most terrible things we can do, it is an "unforgivable sin."[13] I am afraid that this has, unfortunately, happened many times in the past, and it still happens today.

All this striving for freedom can be explained by the longing for this universal unity. Nevertheless, some NDErs stress that longing for universal unity is not about trying to create a boring uniformity. Heaven is no unity blob. Diversity is not extinguished. In the unity universe, there is a lot of diversity in energy. We have to accept that diversity lovingly. Moreover, it has a function. It gives joy to creation. Out of many, we are *one*.

"I gained a clear insight into everything being ONE; everything comes from one source. Struggle and duality are a pitiful waste of energy. 'LOVE' and 'UNITY' and 'SHARING' will bring us 'JOY,' 'WARMTH,' and 'BEING.'"

~Marga van Lennep-Kernkamp

CHAPTER 4

THE IMPORTANCE OF YOU BEING IN THIS UNITY UNIVERSE

"Everything has a purpose. The world is right as it is. It is very well constructed. We don't know what we are supposed to do, but we have a purpose."

~RECURRING STATEMENT OF NDERS

If everything is so beautiful in that other part of the unity universe, then why are we here? Why do we choose to be restricted in this four space-time dimensional world and suffer from all the structures in it, which we partly create ourselves? What, for heaven's sake, are we doing in this vale of tears?

According to NDErs the answer is supposed to be very simple and very easy to comprehend, but not here, not in this extremely restrictive four-dimensional world of ours. Here, we will never really find a conclusive answer. We will get answers the very moment we arrive in the world of The Light. Then we will fully appreciate the reason for our choice to be here, because it is our own choice to be here in the four space-time dimensions, to live in this body, to accept duality, and to adopt a unique personality that is separated from others. Maybe it is better to talk about remembering the reason for choosing to have all kinds of experiences, including a specific set of problems that create real challenges for us. We seem to do time on earth voluntarily. Moreover, we will agree with how everything is put together, because we will discover that the unity universe which includes our world is much more spectacular than any work of man, and that it is very well constructed as it is.

If we choose our life voluntarily, then there must be a good reason. Maybe a full answer to our question is not possible (and don't trust anyone who says he or she is capable of giving a comprehensive answer), but partial answers may be found. Some of the related questions are: Do we have a free will? If The Light is so powerful, then why didn't It create a nice place for everyone to live in but, instead, a place where many wicked things happen?

Everyone has a task

A question I asked many NDErs is whether we have a task. Apparently that was an easy question, because most of them answered affirmative. This coincides with the essence of Hinduism: We all have a task. NDErs do not always have a clear idea of what their task is, but they always know they are here for a good reason. One even said, "Yeah! No one would be here unless we have a task! You experience something yourself, or you help someone to experience something." Therefore, let's conclude that everyone has an important task.

Some NDErs were explicitly made aware of the reason they are on earth. During their experience, they had suddenly been stopped and were not allowed to go any further. They were told to go back to their body in order to finish their tasks. However, after they went back, most NDErs did not have the faintest idea what their particular tasks might be. But they know for sure that there is an important meaning to their life.

It also seems that these tasks have been predetermined before we were born. In some accounts, where NDErs did not want to go back, they were not only told or shown what the reason is for their existence, but they were also made aware that, before they were born, they had promised to perform a specific task. They had voluntarily agreed to and assumed that specific task. When they remembered their agreement, they finally decided to go back to earth. However, when they were revived and came around, they rarely remember what it precisely is. They are sure about having one or more tasks, but simply can't remember them anymore.[1]

This is illustrated in the case of a person who was taken to the hospital after having been assaulted. During his NDE, he heard a voice telling him, "It is not your time to be here, but you may stay if you choose. I have work for you if you choose to return." The NDEr went on to say, "I didn't want to leave, but when the VOICE speaks, you obey. I know I was given a choice, and I chose the pain and misery of earthly life over the absence of all but peace. I sometimes wonder about that choice, but I think I made that choice long before it was put in front of me. I know I have work to do, that's why I came back. I just hope I am ready when the time comes."[2]

Sometimes, when the NDEr refuses to go back, their task would be revealed. They would, for instance, be shown what situations they would be in, what people they would meet, and how that would fit in the broader picture. It would become clear how important the fulfillment of the task would be for all people involved, and for universe as a whole. And after they went back to their body to resume living their lives, these people would sometimes suddenly remember what was shown to them when a certain situation would emerge, or when a specific person would be met.

Whatever our task may be, we must always do it ourselves. No one else should fulfill our task because that would not really be fulfilling. It is absolutely crucial that everyone attends to his or her own duties. For example, during his NDE, a person had a life review with a discussion about his life. He thought that his life was of no use to anyone. He was sure he had failed to use the opportunities he had received in life and felt that there would not be any second chances. Then, in that discussion, he realized all the things he wanted to experience. He wanted to be here, to be human, to be alive (which is very much different from just existing). He said, "I saw the woman I most loved and adored, realized how I yearned to experience that love; to move through life with her, to experience everything I could with her. I instantly knew how and why I wanted to impact the world, what part I wanted to play in giving to the world. Making my contribution, leaving my mark, and the true motivations behind them. How I could, and why only I could in the way I could. Why those things are unique to me. And not for any of the reasons I might have guessed. I realized that within me there are reasons, and emotions, and motivations I had never before given myself credit for."[3]

Tasks may not be something important in the earthly sense, but it is always something important to the unity universe. It could be sweeping streets or crunching numbers, but it could also be something else, like raising kids or learning to deal with ailing parents. Some examples of tasks of the people I spoke to are nursing people (one NDEr told me that her task in the 1980s was to work specifically with people with

AIDS), looking after other people's children, raising children, showing people how to be positive, being on the board
of a specific society, and also someone who had to make
people aware that the war in Iraq should not be started,
and after it had started, that it should be stopped as soon
as possible. And at the age of four when she had her first
NDE in the concentration camp in Indonesia, Tienke knew
that she had to write a book. She was absolutely sure about
it, even though at that time, she didn't know how to write.
Moreover, there was neither education nor paper to help her
on her way.

We should also know that it may not be just one task we
have, but several. In any case, our tasks are there to contribute
to the world, to nature, and to the lives of ourselves and others. This is confirmed consistently in NDEs. A clear example
is an NDEr who explicitly asked why we are on earth. The
answer was, "You are here on earth for one reason. You're only
here to help each other."[4] This implies another important
thing. Everyone is valuable in this big plan. The president of
the United States of America or the queen of the Netherlands
may seem very important according to earthly measures, but
it is stressed time and again that all of us are involved in this
great scheme and that everyone is equally important. There are
no lesser souls. The president and the queen whom we cheer as
they pass by are just as important in this world as the beggar we
ignore in the street, or the refugee we deny to participate in our
wealth. So, yes, everyone has a good reason to be here.

When we are convinced of this truth, another question becomes important: Do we have the free will to fulfill our tasks?

Free will? Yes

This was another question that I asked everyone, but this question was not as easy as the previous one. There was slightly more doubt with NDErs about the answer to the question of whether we have free will. One started telling me that we don't have free will at all. After all, she felt as if she had no choice in coming back to earth or staying in that blissful environment. But later she told me that she had agreed to being born on earth in this particular family to give her father the opportunity not to abuse her. Apparently, she agreed that there is free will.

Others say that we don't have free will in neglecting or even avoiding our task. You may try, but it will not feel good. After all, before you were born, you decided for yourself to attend to that specific task. And apparently the world is organized in such a way that you will find a manner to succeed. Some said that we have no choice in going from A to B, because B defines the fulfillment of our task, but there is a choice in the road we take from A to B.

This freedom relates especially to the emotions you display. Sad things happen to everyone, and in the case of Silvia, a singer and performer radiating a lot of energy, there were a lot of problems with her health. Her body would not do what it was supposed to do and doctors couldn't find the reason.

After many partially successful operations, she was left with a colostomy. Because of her NDE, she now understands that she does not have a choice there. Her poor health and the colostomy were predetermined to happen. However, she did have a choice in emotions. There were options. She could sit down in a corner and feel utterly sad, for which she had every reason, but she could also choose another emotion. She decided to try to go for it and to show her environment that, even with a colostomy, she can be radiant.

She is not the only one who told me that we have a choice in how to deal with situations. Perhaps situations cannot change, but we have options how to respond. Positive, joyful, and accepting responses have an energy-increasing effect in the universe, as do consciousness-enhancing responses, while negative, sad, hateful, rejecting, and truth-denying responses have an energy-shrinking effect. Our responses create energy that ripples through the world. Probably without knowing it, in choosing our response, we become creative. We can create, and in that sense, we are co-creators of The Light. That is one of the essences of the Jewish religion: God created the universe in six days; the seventh day He rests and it becomes our turn to create.

So, when it comes to fulfilling our task, we seem to have limited room for maneuver. Nevertheless, there is one rigorous way in which we can choose to avoid fulfillment. It is called suicide. While attending an IANDS conference in Houston, someone in an experiencer panel told how he had once felt utterly useless.[5] He had combined a lot of alcohol with a lot of speed, and at a certain point in time, he became convinced that his life insurance was worth more than his life. When he was rosy enough, he took his car and sped into a solid wall. He miraculously survived. During his NDE in the operating room, he could see everything the doctors did. He had 360-degree vision. But there was much more to see; and from that he became astounded by the effect of his act. He saw it ripple through time.

He said what many other NDErs say, that everything has a purpose, and that the world is right as it is. It is very well-constructed. We don't know what we are supposed to do, but we all have a purpose. Therefore, no one is useless.

He was given a choice to go back, and his answer was wholeheartedly yes! Immediately he returned, and he was glad to be back, even though he looked like Frankenstein after all the necessary surgery.

Another person who attempted suicide described the effect of her attempt as follows:[6] "My mind became acutely aware of the pain and suffering born out of my choice of self-destruction...how my actions were like stones tossed into a pond. They rippled out, crossing over the entire surface of the earth, forever affecting and changing the face of it."

She also mentioned that she saw and felt the effects of all her actions throughout her life. Moreover, she saw and felt all the options she had been given in life. She saw what she could have done differently, which probably included an alternative to suicide.

She then saw a place where other people are who had committed suicide. She can sense how these people are stuck somewhere in their feelings of the pain they caused others through their selfish choices. She says that she doesn't know whether there is a hell, but that this suffering that people created themselves was more than hell. God doesn't need to create a place to make us suffer for wasting wonderful opportunities; apparently we can do that perfectly well ourselves.

Like others, she concludes that life is a gift. It should be gratefully accepted. The purpose of this gift is to have many experiences, even though some of them might not be such happy ones. They give opportunities to learn about love. And of course we will make mistakes; how else can we learn? But we need problems and we need to fail once in a while so that we learn the essence of love. Remember that love, in the broadest sense, is mentioned time and again by NDErs as the single-most important thing there is. So in a way, we have to be grateful for the problems we encounter in our lives, and give our best in trying to solve them in a loving way.

Free will? No

We seem to have a task which we agree upon before we are born. Therefore, we seem to be destined to go from A to B, since B determines the fulfillment of our task. We don't have a choice there. However, sometimes things seem to be fixed in even greater detail. Some people, notably many NDErs after their experience, know what is going to happen in the future, and are able to predict the future. They know even seemingly insignificant details before they happen. So what does that tell us? Are we free to decide which road we will take to go from A to the fulfillment of our task that lies in B, or is even the road predetermined?

To a certain degree, we do have free will to determine our road. This was confirmed by many NDErs. There should be another reason for the fact that some people can correctly tell the future. The solution may be hidden in the remarkable aspect of time. Remember that in the unity universe, all time exists at once. Everything is now. The past, the present and the future are the same. They blend. Seeing history and the future at the same time can be likened to sitting in an airplane when you are able to see two different cities at the same time.

This means that where that blending of time occurs, some-one would be able to see what the outcome is of a choice we are about to make. They would be seeing us in the morning wavering between our options, and at the same time see what decision we have arrived at in the evening. People who are able to predict the future, may be able to tap into this knowledge. Remember that NDErs who have that ability still have an open door to this other part of the unity universe where this blending of time occurs.

Another way of looking at free will was offered several times during my interviews. It is a very interesting point of view, and one that may be of great importance to our world. I understood that "free will" actually is a concept that applies to our four-dimensional world, but not to the other part of unity universe. When NDErs are asked about free will, they have a problem relating to it.

I have been assured by different NDErs that, seen from the spirit world, a free will is not required. The universe is guiding us. Everyone has an internal compass, and not following it is a waste of time. It helps us fulfill our tasks, because we are destined to achieve our goal. We just have to be aligned and in tune with The Light, and all will go smoothly. One NDEr even got emotional when I continuously asked her about free will. She said, "In that other dimension, free will is not important. It is important here, because it is related to man, to the ego of man, but I want to go with the universal flow. I don't want my free will to be in discord with universe. I don't want it to be in the way of my fulfillment."

However, she stressed explicitly that her attitude had nothing to do with a lack of will. She said that sitting in a chair, waiting for universe to get her going was not what she meant. What it meant to her is not to put her ego first. In her NDE, she had to let go of her ego, and that was what had felt right. Here, on earth again, she tries to let go as well. This coincides with the essence of Buddhism: We have to let go of our ego. We have to discard the Self.

Our four-dimensional world is part of the unity universe. Therefore, it should be beneficial to be in tune with the The Light in this unity universe. It enhances energy; it will make us more loving and it will eventually make us happier. Not being in tune will make us feel bad, unhappy, and out of place, and in extreme cases, we will get ill. It is just like being in love. We can resist it, but that will hurt tremendously.

The same applies to society as a whole. We can go against the nature of The Light, but that will eventually harm humanity. We can try to fight it and impose our will. Maybe, at first, it will seem to work, and it might look as if we get our way. But in the end, we will discover that The Light is much stronger and that our battle has damaged only us.

All of this points in the direction that we should exercise our free will to be aligned with The Light. By doing so, we in fact voluntarily waive the use of ego's free will. We discard the Self. Actually, this is what is meant in the Lord's Prayer when we say, "Yours will be done." And this is also the meaning of the word Muslim: the one who submits himself to Allah/God.

Positive ripples

So the preliminary conclusion is that we all are extremely valuable because we all have an important task to fulfill. To a certain degree, we have a free will, but the easiest way to achieve our goal is to voluntarily waive free will and choose to be aligned with The Light. The question that arises now is: If The Light is so powerful, then why didn't It create a nice place for everyone to live in, but, instead, this vale of tears where the most terrible things happen?

First, we have to remember that The Light is unconditional love, and that It doesn't take pleasure in hurting people. Neither does It have enjoyment when we suffer pain, are hungry or unwell, or when a misfortune strikes us. Although some people insist otherwise, it is not true that misery and setbacks exist as a kind of punishment for what we previously did wrong in our current life, or perhaps even in a previous one. Hurricane Katrina (and subsequently Rita), which caused so much destruction and sorrow in New Orleans in 2005 are not punishment from The Light. Nor are earthquakes, tsunamis, or the current financial and economic crisis. The Light does not punish. Manmade misery and setbacks should also not be considered as a punishment from The Light.

The worst example of manmade misery is war. According to an NDEr who explicitly asked about it, war is not what The Light wants.[7] It dislikes war. That war occurs, and The Light allows it to occur, because it is the result of the free will of people. When enough people desire it, war can take place, but The Light still detests it. It is against Its nature, because Its nature is one of total and unconditional love. War is the ultimate example of man's free will not being aligned with The Light. And needless to say, war is quite damaging, and causes great sorrow on both sides. Another example of the effect of non-alignment is the current financial and economic crisis (see Chapter 8).

Misery, pain, sorrow, and all kinds of setbacks don't exist to thwart us. The only reason why this occurs is to give us the opportunity to make choices. When everything would be perfect and things would always run smoothly, the only serious choice we would have each day would be, for instance, what kind of vegetables to eat for dinner. However, when things are imperfect and problems arise, the range of options increases. The more choices we have, the more opportunities exist for us to learn about love, and to develop compassion for people.[8] In fact, problems challenge us to choose the most optimal alternative.

Of course, our choices do not always lead us to a solution, and sometimes there is no solution at all to a specific problem, but it is not about reaching a solution. It is about the way in which we deal with the problem; it is about our reaction to the problem; it is about the emotions we choose to have. Our choice of intentions when we do something is particularly important. All of this determines the route we take to go from A to B. It is destined that we arrive at B, but from the road we choose, we can derive the measure of our compassion. Moreover, along the road, we get a lot of choices, which are opportunities to grow our compassion.

Remember the life review in Chapter 2 of the woman who was helping her school friend to get rid of the lice. At the start, A, we have a school friend with lice. At the finish, B, a school friend without lice. There is no choice in the goal, but only in the routes we take from start to finish. There are at least two routes. Route one: Make a fuss by drawing everyone's attention to the itchy creatures. The choice to act in a loveless way humiliated the school friend. Route two: Take the school friend aside and silently work on the problem. This would have brought loving comfort to the school friend and harmony to both.

Many NDErs say that there are always several honorable alternatives in which quiet and peace are possible. They are sometimes difficult to realize, but they are there. An NDEr said that The Light showed her alternate scenes. "These were solutions which would have allowed for peace, while still honoring myself. Futhermore, honorable solutions, while often seeming most difficult, bring the greatest soul growth to all involved. And I saw that one of the major purposes for relationships on earth was to support and facilitate soul growth."[9]

The Light made her aware that we have to find out how to do this. For any problem in our life we should try to find the most optimal solution, which means a solution that increases compassion in the world.

Our choices affect the unity universe and the energy in it. Throughout the day we constantly choose. We choose our emotions, we choose our thoughts, we choose what to do, and sometimes what not to do. All our emotions, thoughts, and actions have an effect on the world. For instance, Betty Eadie said that if we knew the power of our thoughts, we would be more careful. She knows this from her interesting and extensive NDE, which she relayed in her best-selling book. Another NDEr said, "I know that our actions affect others in both positive and negative ways and that we will come to appreciate this fact in the next place."[10] And many more NDErs will confirm this extremely important, but grossly undervalued truth.

Remember, emotions such as hatred, anger, fear, unfriendliness, intolerance, egoism, despair, despondency, and greed create negative vibrations.[11] There is a fair chance that they will have an adverse affect on our own lives. Part of all our illnesses is created by us. However, we have to understand that our negative emotions also create negative ripples that run through the world. These don't stop with the parties involved. Their effect goes beyond and because they cause total energy to shrink, they affect people even in places we don't know or will never visit during our lifetime.

Fortunately, something similar applies to positive emotions, such as love, patience, trust, friendliness, tolerance, charity, hope, generosity, and kindness. These create positive ripples. And apart from the probability that they have a beneficial effect on us, these ripples also travel around the world to places we never dreamed of. Likewise, in a positive way, they will affect people we don't know, and probably will never see. When you bring joy to one soul, millions will receive this vibration. Because these positive emotions increase energy and love, they even bring joy to the unity universe.

Gratitude is an absolutely important, positive emotion. We should take nothing for granted. Look around and see where we are and what we have. We should be grateful for being alive, for having sufficient food, a roof over our head, and clean drinking water. We have a toilet, and we flush it with water! We should be grateful to have people around us whom we can decide to like, or maybe even to love. Likewise, we should be grateful for

the people around us who decide to like us, or maybe even
to love us. We should even be grateful for the obstacles in
our life, because they give us the opportunity to grow love by
choosing a loving reaction. In that sense, we should also love
our enemies.

No resignation, but serve!

In some circumstances, it is difficult to be grateful, such as
in the case of an illness or the loss of a loved one. In these, and
many other cases, it would be a bit odd to be grateful. However,
perhaps later, with hindsight, one might find out why things
went as they did, and one might eventually appreciate the
course of those events, too.

When we have no possibility to change the situation,
acceptance is the only thing that remains. In these cases, it
is important to be confident that everything happens for a
good reason. This is what NDErs are very certain of. They
saw how very well our world with everything in it is constructed, and how well it forms a part of the unity universe.
For non-NDErs, it is more difficult to see how this is. With
our limited focus on the four-dimensions, we are insufficiently
equipped to fully appreciate that truth. Therefore, the only
thing we can do is to have confidence that all is well. Don't be
afraid of living. We have to trust that everything has a good
purpose in the universe. And we should trust that everyone is
helped. If we are aligned with The Light, we will be led to our
destiny, which will be most fulfilling from the point of view
of the unity universe.

If you're convinced that passive resignation to a severe loss is sufficient, you're almost there. A slightly further advance is possible. One NDEr told me that the resignation doesn't have to be passive. If there is pain, acknowledge that pain. Don't cherish it, but realize that it is there, look at it, and allow it to be there. Another NDEr said that we should live our highs but also our lows. When we do that, we take away the extra burden that the loss causes and it will give some energy. Then it is not a passive process anymore; it becomes a bit more dynamic because we actively acknowledge the pain.

Actively acknowledging the pain may still not be the most optimal situation. For instance, when there is an irreversible loss, one would still have moments thinking, "Okay, I accept it, but why did it happen to me? What should I do now? How should I go on? How can I continue living?"

In these cases, it is best to realize that we are interconnected in a very profound and spiritual way. This means that it is very beneficial to ourselves when we create positive ripples. These are best created when we serve others. So look around and see what we can do, and where we can serve. Where can we help someone else? Where can we add something positive to our environment? It doesn't have to be big or world reforming. It may very well be something small or seemingly insignificant. If we look around to find something to do, we will be astonished to find enough to do in our own vicinity. At the very least, we could give a smile to the neighbor or to the other people we see during the day, or even to the beggar in the street. But we could also just spend time with friends or family, walking in a park or preparing dinner together. And we could also decide to do something such as voluntary work, such as looking after that beggar, or clearing away the waste in our street. Make that street look clean again! But in whichever way we choose to serve, we should be able to feel the interconnection with each other, with nature, and even with The Light.

We have to keep in mind that positive acts are beneficial to everyone, including us. Service makes people happy: those whom we serve, and also the one who serves. Service binds the love in us. And by doing this, we create positive ripples, even when we suffered a loss. We have to constantly realize that the power lies within our own minds. So, we should create only good vibrations, at all times, even when it seems dark. After all, we are responsible for the energy we create. Be sure it is the positive kind.

CHAPTER 5

FORGIVENESS IS AN ACT OF LOVE

Living in the Now

Living in the now

In the silence

between your thoughts

you will meet

God's thoughts

your intuition,

the rest are details

~FRANS TOMEIJ[1]

When he regained consciousness after his NDE, he immediately thought of Einstein's words: "I want to know God's thoughts, the rest are details." Later, he wrote this poem.

We all influence the world in an invisible way. Each of our thoughts and emotions has power, and it ripples through our four-dimensional world and beyond. In the previous chapter, a number of positive emotions were mentioned, such as patience, trust, friendliness, tolerance, charity, hope, generosity, and kindness. In fact, these are different forms of love. From all NDEs, it becomes very clear that love is the most important thing in the universe. It is the building block of everything, not only in that invisible other world, but also of all the material things we find in our world. In fact, what you think matters; in fact, it forms matter.

Love expands energy in the same way that hatred and other negative emotions make it shrink. However, negative vibrations can be stopped. They can be neutralized. This happens when they meet love. A specific form of love is forgiveness. It is an important form of love, but it needs a little bit more explanation. In this chapter, some examples of the importance of forgiveness will be given. The principal example is the one of Desirée, a dear friend of mine, who likes to think of everyone as an angel, because in her NDE, she saw that she is an angel herself.

Desirée's story

As a baby, Desirée had some problems with her skin. It was painful eczema, and at times, it would hurt so much, that she would cry. Once it annoyed her mother so much that she firmly pressed a pillow to Desirée's face. Desirée knows this from her life review, which she had during her NDE some 30 years later.

During this life review, she saw how, as a baby, she had left her body, and from an elevated point of view, had seen what her mother was doing. When her mother took the pillow away, she was able to breathe again, and instantly returned to her body. Desirée was amazed that she was able to see something that had happened when she was a baby, because normally people don't remember anything before the age of three or four. Nevertheless, she distinctly felt the safety of getting out of her body. Apparently the event and the feelings were still there.

When she was three years old and couldn't yet look over the edge of the bathtub, her father started to have sex with her. It would often happen during showering, but he would occasionally take her into her parents' bedroom. Sometimes it would be too much for her to take, and just like the pillow moment in the cradle, she would escape from her body. She knows about this because she had also seen it in her life review. In the safety of her out-of-body experience, she could see what her father was doing to her. After a while, he would notice that Desirée was not responding, and to bring her around, he would shower her with cold water. That was a nasty way to get her back in her body again.

Because she was quite young when the incest started, she thought it was normal. Her mother knew, because sometimes she too would join them in the shower or in the bedroom. Incidentally, other male relatives would sometimes be involved.

Suddenly, when she was 11, it all stopped. She had to take showers alone and no one in the family would ever touch her again. Desirée grew up developing a feeling that she was worthless. Materially, she had no reason to complain, because she had everything she wanted. She had her own bedroom with many toys, and she went on luxurious vacations with her parents. But in her heart there was tremendous pain.

Her NDEs

At times, the pain in her heart became unbearable. Once, when she was 31, she was cycling with a friend when the pain exploded. She stopped cycling and put her bike aside just in time before she had her heart attack. The ambulance came, and she remembered going in and out of her body while the ambulance sped to the hospital.

There she had her first NDE. At an incredible speed, she was propelled into an all embracing Light. It was shining white, almost like snow glittering in the sun. She hadn't seen anything else like that in her whole life. It was wonderful. It was brilliant. It was reassuring. She was one with it. It was all around her, but it also went through her. It was in her. She experienced The Light in every possible way, as if she was seeing, feeling, tasting, hearing, and smelling It, but it was more than that. It was as if she had more than those five senses. And she felt unconditional love. It felt eternal, but it was not like the end of all, it was more like winding up for a new beginning. But suddenly, there was this voice that said she had to go back again. With the same speed of light, she returned to her body.

The doctors couldn't find anything alarming—no heart attack, only an insignificant flutter. They sent her home the same evening. Still, during the next two weeks, everything seemed wrong to her. She couldn't remember names, she couldn't speak in correct sentences, she couldn't see properly, her left arm was not doing what she ordered it to do, and on top of all that, she felt intensely tired. She was not functioning normally at all.

Regularly, she would find herself out of her body. She would see herself lying on the couch, where she had fallen asleep or had become unconscious. She tried to command herself to get up, but she couldn't make her body move. She seemed to have lost control. While floating above her body, she could sometimes even drift so far away that she could see the rooftops in her neighborhood, as if she was hanging somewhere above her house. At one time, when she thought it would be better to die, she saw two magnificent beings standing at her bed. She looked at them with her eyes open. They were clearly not human; could they be angels? "We will take you with us to that other world, further through that Light you experienced before."

Desirée felt that her soul structure got intertwined with that of both angels, and this time she had the feeling of a more controlled out-of-body experience. She saw that the eyes of her physical body were closed, and noticed that there was hardly any respiration. The rhythm of her heart slowed. Then the three of them left through the ceiling, leaving the body behind. Just like the first time, again at the speed of light, she shot through a kind of tunnel. While in this tunnel, she felt more and more of a unity with both angels. She was grateful for being accompanied in her NDE by them.

Suddenly, she saw a city in the distance, and from non-verbal communication with the two angels, she felt that they would take her to Christ. He would have something important to tell her. They went to a particularly beautiful building, a palace, very pure and colorful, like crystal. There were other beings of wonderful light, just like her two angels. In fact, she realized that she was the same. She was also an angel when she was not on earth.

In that building she met well-known spiritual figures, such as Ghandi, Osho, Mohammed, and Lao Tse. They were very kind to her, and started a conversation with her about what she could do in her life.

Next, a splendid being emerged from one of the corridors whom she immediately recognized as Christ. He moved behind her and while he did that, the palace and all in it disappeared. It was like turning on the light to suddenly see a completely different environment.

The show she was about to see was her life, but also the period immediately before. She saw how she accompanied an angel to be born on earth, and she realized that this soul was destined to become her husband later in her life. Then she saw how she herself was accompanied by other angels to be born. She saw that she had agreed to be raised in that particular family to give her father the opportunity to choose not to abuse her.

She had known that it was going to be a painful experience when he would not choose to stay away from her, but her anxiousness to feel how it is to be on earth was greater. She remembered that she didn't pay too much attention to the possibility of pain, but instead was thrilled to experience life.

She witnessed her own birth, her mother with the pillow, her father in the shower choosing the less optimal alternative.... She saw the other male relatives, and the struggle she had with her body throughout the greater part of her life. But she also saw her vacations, her study, her sensitivity and intuition, her friends, and all the other nice experiences in her life. In the meantime, Christ said that he understood her pain. After all, he knew the feeling.

Next, he showed her the start of creation, how consciousness is a part of it, and that earth is just a small particle of the whole universe. He mentioned that she should read the Vedas and the Bhagavat-Gita. In his opinion, Christians could go well with other religions. She understood this to mean that all religions and cultures could form an interesting puzzle for humanity to put together and to learn from. They shouldn't be seen as adversaries. Rather, they should be like each other's addition, because together, they have surplus value.

Subsequently, he showed major events in Desirée's life, the important people who would turn up in it, and the significant tasks she has. She saw that she would have the opportunity to work in Africa, that she would finally meet her husband, that her mother would have cancer, and so on. He also explained the importance of forgiveness, and that profound love flows from it when it happens. Then he asked whether she could be able to forgive those who traumatized her. And in the presence of his unconditional love she said wholeheartedly, "Yes, I can."

He then went on to say, "Never ask anyone to forgive on your behalf, because you can do it yourself. Others will voluntarily follow you, as will people who haven't had an experience like yours."

It meant that her forgiveness would induce others to do the same thing. They too would be able to forgive in a similar way. She saw it happen. She saw it spread around. Her act of love would be beneficial to the world, not because Desirée was such an important soul, but because every act of love is important. Each of them spreads far beyond the directly involved. She also noticed that the beneficial effect would return to her as well.

After receiving that important piece of knowledge, the two angels accompanied her back to earth. They helped her to make contact with her body and, finally, to become one with it again. Then the angels let go of her soul structure so that they would be separated from her again.

A kick in the butt

If you think that after this experience her life became much easier, you are dead wrong. It took two full years to recover from being reduced from the wonderful expanded being of light to this tight body form with its limited capabilities. Some NDErs even need more time to accept that they are "earthlings" again with all sorts of handicaps and restrictions (see Chapter 10). Besides, she had to recover physically, because, for instance, her eyes didn't work well and her arms still would not take any of her commands. At first, she was afraid that she would become blind, but after a while, her sight came back. Last, but not least, she had to learn to cope with her traumas. Even though she had promised to forgive, her traumas were still there to the full extent. After all, she was still a regular human being.

After months, when she could finally go back to work, her boss started to intimidate her sexually. At first, she tried to cope with it, like most people probably would. She tried to avoid the remarks and see the humor of it. But the situation got worse when her colleagues sided with her boss. Remembering her promise, she turned to her parents for support. However, they ridiculed her, not only about the sexual harassment, but also about her NDE. "Just go see another psychiatrist again, you did often enough before."

Desirée exploded. That was just one of their little games to humiliate her. They just continued with what they had always done, but this time it was more than she could take. She decided never to see them again. In addition, Desirée took sick leave. She also took legal steps to sue her boss, a huge struggle that lasted many years, but turned out positive for her. And she decided on something else, on something more important.

She decided not to get stuck in her feeling of misery. She had seen how beautiful she is, and how much love there is in universe. She wanted to do something positive, and therefore, as a paramedic, she was going to develop a treatment for people with indefinable pain problems. After all, her own heart pains had made her an expert in this field. Moreover, during her NDE, she had received a lot of information on possible treatments, and she was definitely going to try putting hers into practice.

More than a year went by when she received a shocking letter from her parents. It was established that her mother had cancer and would require some aggressive medical treatment. Her parents pleaded with her to help them through the chemotherapy. Desirée was in doubt. What to do? They had never helped her, so why would she help them now? After all, they were the ones who had treated her maliciously and had let her down all her life.

She sat down to meditate. While calming down, she realized again that she was here to show forgiveness. She had promised it. Moreover, being in that family had been of her own accord. Therefore, she had to follow her heart and go back to her parents. She suddenly also understood that the sexual harassment by her boss could be seen as an extra wake-up call for her parents. "Hey parents, I am talking about incest. That is what you did to me, remember?! That is even worse than sexual harassment!" They had missed this wake-up call and the chance to come to terms with what they had done, but now there was another chance: cancer.

It was a painful decision, but she went to her parents. This time, however, she was strong. She had nothing to lose. She was not dependent on her parents anymore. In fact, she had never been. She was an angel, a fantastic being of light, and no sexual harassment or abuse could ever have changed that. When she followed her heart and listened to universe, she would not suffer from heart pains any more.

This time she made sure the message was clear. "I literally kicked him in the butt; and through his trousers I squeezed his [testicles] hard. I screamed, 'Now you must finally recognize what you did to me! You will not play it down any more!'"

There are alternatives

This story shows that the process of forgiving her parents was long and painful. An important part of that process was that Desirée had to understand who she really is. She had to be really conscious of it. She was a victim, and she had no choice there, because as a small child, she could not avoid that awful situation. Like other children, she had been dependent on her parents in a material way. But being a victim and not being able to escape from it was not the important part of her. She had to become conscious of the fact that spiritually, she was already a most wonderful being because she was related to The Light. She had to realize that the core of her being is The Light, and as such, she already had everything she needed.

In the next phase of the process of forgiveness, she had to gain self-respect. This meant that she had to have respect for the divine light within herself and find ways to express it. It required that she would start to love herself and see that she is of great value, no matter what her parents did to her or tried to make her believe. In addition, she had to understand that she is capable of doing positive things with her life and to create positive ripples. And she did that by developing a treatment for people with indefinable pain problems, which she has successfully used in her new job.

This self-realization was very important to her, but it was insufficient to change the relationship with her parents. Something else was needed. She had a choice in her emotions. She could continue to be the offended child and cease to have contact with her parents. It would mean leaving the situation as it was: unclear, untidy, a status quo, and she would be continuing a situation with heart pains lingering in the background. Or, she could stop feeling that the most important aspect in her life was being a victim.

She chose to go over to them and to make them conscious, too. They needed a real understanding of what they did, and as such, it may be likened to what happens during a life review. During life reviews, people are made aware of what they did to others, not to punish them, but in order for them to gain a better understanding of the different opportunities they had in creating love. Likewise, Desirée's parents needed insight and a true understanding of their actions. They had to rise above their egos. Only then would the situation be really cleared, and create positive energy for all involved. Bringing about that consciousness is what she did in an interesting, physical way.

We can find something similar in the NDE of a woman who was brought up in a dysfunctional family.[2] During her life review, she started to feel what every single one of her relatives had felt during their lives. She explicitly states that her relatives weren't mean and abusive on purpose, but rather that they were over-powered by what they encountered daily. Every day, they experienced a vast lack of love and compassion around them, and how people treated them unfairly. There was no one to lead with a good example and to show how to give a reaction with love rather than with aggression. There simply was no role model.

Having a clear picture of how her relatives were trapped in their own behavior and couldn't really change things made her feel true compassion toward each of them. It brought true forgiveness. This forgiveness was healing, because when she came back to earth, she no longer felt the acute pain of the abuse from her childhood. All her resentment had vanished.

There was more to her story than compassion and forgiveness. Interestingly, during her life review, she was asked a very important question. She was asked how she had honored the Divine Light within herself. The question made her realize who she really is. She is a True Child of God, as she puts it herself, with a responsibility to honor that gift. That applies to everyone else as well, because she saw how valuable everybody is. "There are no 'lesser' souls."

Most of us are brought up with the notion to respect and honor others. However, we often forget that this applies to ourselves too: We also have to respect and honor ourselves. The reason is that, in essence, we are the spark of The Light that is within us. If we don't honor ourselves, we show disrespect to The Light. Therefore, we should try not to allow others to misuse us or to mistreat us physically or mentally. In some cases that would be very difficult, perhaps even impossible.

Nevertheless, we should try not to be passive, but to look for honorable solutions for everyone. By actively trying, we already show our respect for The Light.

The woman was shown that there were alternatives for each family member. They could go on treating each other in a nasty and abusive way. However, they could also become conscious of their situation, tap into their inner feelings, connect and align with The Light within them, and let love change the course of their lives.

We often think that we do not have alternatives to our current way of living. Helped by our parents, relatives, and teachers, our lives seem to have unfolded in a particular direction. We are formed by all sorts of events, which help the ego to develop and be on solid ground. And the painful events especially can have the effect of freezing us in an unpleasant situation that we think we cannot change. We become used to this unpleasant situation, which sometimes develops into something worse. And even then, we have the amazing ability to get used to it. How often do women stay with their abusive men, rather than run away? The abusive situation is safe because it is known to them, while running away opens up a lot of uncertainty.

We think we are restrained by what happened in the past and, therefore, we allow the fixation in certain roles to happen. The ego is caught up in fixed patterns and role-playing. This is the only way it can demonstrate that it exists. By continuously performing its role, the ego continues its existence.

However, more often than we think, there are honorable alternatives, in which quiet and peace are possible. They may not be easy to realize, and sometimes they may seem impossible, but we have to try. And when we actually realize one of these alternatives, and leap out of our negative fixation, it brings spiritual growth for all parties involved. The NDEr from the dysfunctional family said that she could see how people could grow when they moved away from their acquired reflexes to cause pain or aggression and, instead, gave a response with love and compassion. She also saw how love and compassion from non-involved parties could facilitate positive changes in the lives of the involved parties.[3]

Remember who you really are

After their experiences, NDErs have an open connection with the realm of The Light. The stairway to heaven occasionally opens up to them without them having to go through a life-threatening medical crisis again. In her life, Tienke, who wrote a beautiful book about both NDEs, has had several opportunities to climb the stairway again. After one of these occasions, she returned with a particular sentence ringing in her head: Evil is nothing other than good that doesn't know itself.[4]

She explains that everyone has a core of The Light within. Circumstances in which people grow up may cause some pollution. Sometimes the pollution is so massive that it completely obscures The Light from shining through. It is the "strangulation of the soul," as she calls it.

Just think of the many people on earth, most of them amassed in big cities, who have no compassionate role models. It is awful when children are given the wrong examples and grow up thinking it is normal to beat up one's wife, to have incest with one's children, to steal from one's neighbors, to go about pulling one's gun, to sell mortgages to people whom we know will never be able to pay the interest (the notorious sub-primes). All of this is not in alignment with the nature of The Light.

In Desirée's case, she saw that she had The Light within, but also that her father has The Light within. His Light had been obscured because he too had had a wrong role model and was gravely affected by it. He had also been sexually abused at a young age, which polluted his inner core. Therefore, in the first place, it is really absolutely necessary that we all become conscious of our situation and what effect we have on others. If we have lived in a loveless way, we have to become aware of it. It is a necessary first step toward improvement.

We shouldn't wait for the kick in the butt, but we should try to open our eyes ourselves. We should try to be open to the criticism of others or for other signs to make us conscious about what we do. In whatever way obtained, consciousness is a key factor. If we remain unconscious, we are bound to continue what we have been doing before, either as the villain or as the victim. This will cause more pollution that conceals our most wonderful inner core.

Secondly, we shouldn't linger in the pain we felt in times gone by, but we must take advantage of the pristine present moment: the now. Every day, there are zillions of these now-moments. Our consciousness is capable of understanding what is happening in the time-bound four-dimensions, but at the same time, it is capable to step out of time and align with The Light within us. Time and again, NDErs tell how important the present moment is. See, for instance, the poem "Living in the now" at the start of this chapter, written by an NDEr.

Performing this trick of looking in both directions is one of the reasons the now is so important. Living in the now, we can look in both worlds, because our consciousness is eternal and endless. It can understand the mess we are in, and at the same time, align with The Light and remember who we really are. Alignment with The Light means alignment with unconditional love. It is within everyone, sometimes brilliantly visible, but sometimes buried deep within. In any case, it is there.

Finally, we have to see that there are alternatives. Being aligned, we are able to choose the most optimal one, which is the one that gives the best opportunity for everyone to expand love. What has been in the past has gone by. We can't change that anymore. We have to go on. Therefore, we should choose a more loving and more positive road that adds to the energy in the world. Let's rely on our own spark of Light to take us there.

CHAPTER 6

THE TRUTH ABOUT REINCARNATION

"I became more fully aware of the fact that God (our Creator) wants us to experience everything that we wish to experience. Nothing is denied us, only that which we inherently deny ourselves. And while certain experiences do not always lead to pleasant outcomes, they do lead to a certain amount of enlightenment. Especially as one returns his or her thinking to The Light and focuses on God's wish for us to learn a more loving way to live our lives."

~CHRISTIAN ANDRÉASON

Christian had his Near-Death Experience after an accidental overdose of anesthesia while having dental surgery. He is an award-winning recording artist and singer who began an intuitively based, life-coaching practice soon after his 1995 NDE. Since this time, Christian has so-far worked with and counseled thousands of individuals one-on-one.[1]

A significant number of NDErs do not rule out reincarnation, and many of them even started to believe it as a fact of life. During their experiences, some NDErs have seen spirits or beings of light who are enthusiastically awaiting their reincarnation on earth as a baby.[2] This, however, doesn't have to mean that all those spirits were human beings before. It could very well be that spirits go to earth to be incarnated only once, and after their body dies, they return to the spirit world to stay there.

Some of those who believe in reincarnation say they were shown their previous lives, or have even seen their future lives during their NDE. An example is Tienke Klein, who devotes several chapters in her book to the journey of her soul throughout many ages.[3] During the overview she had of her many reincarnations, she became more and more aware of The Light that we all are. She came to a point where she no longer identified with any of the people she had previously been, nor with the personalities these people had in a specific culture at a certain time.

Therefore, perhaps we have to conclude that reincarnation really exists. In that case, there would be all the more reason to be good to one another, to ensure that everyone has enough to eat and drink, and to protect nature. If reincarnation exists, then, in our next earthly life, perhaps we might be reborn as a poor child in one of the gigantic slums of one of the many cities in a developing country. In the next earthly life, we might depend on someone we were very nasty to in this life. And if reincarnation exists, we will return to the environment that we helped to pollute. We will return to a world that we previously left behind with considerably fewer forests, with dirty drinking water, and with a smaller variety of plants and animals.

However, perhaps we have to remember that the other part of the unity universe, where NDErs have been, is so completely new, so spectacular, so not of this world, that with our knowledge it is impossible to understand, let alone to give words to it. This also applies to reincarnation. So while it is clear that reincarnation has a part to play, it remains difficult to be sure about exactly what that is. In a long and deep discussion about the reality of reincarnation, Tienke exclaimed, "Reincarnation exists. Reincarnation doesn't exist. These are conclusions drawn while having an earthly consciousness. Every conclusion about reincarnation drawn in a lower dimension is bound to be incomplete. It is like an apple that has to say something about how it feels to be an orange."

Reincarnation is real

Many NDErs say they have the feeling they have lived before. Some are even absolutely sure about this. One even said that, in her life review, she was taken to the very start of life on earth, millions of years ago, and that she saw how she had been a single-celled organism. She said that it was as if the outline or information of that organism was still in her genetic material. Others merely state that they have witnessed series of their previous lives. "I was shown a long line of experiences in other realms of realities and on other worlds. It was some time later I realized it was my past "lives" review of all existences of which I had been part."[4]

People have the feeling that reincarnation is true, because, for instance, they feel that certain aspects of previous lives have their effect in this life. They feel that we have to have different experiences and have to go through different emotions. Each time, we are given a different set of things to learn. Some also say that we are consulted on what to learn in the next life. There seems to be a choice as well in which experiences we want to have, or which emotions we want to go through. Apparently, most people believe that the reason for reincarnation is to learn and to become more complete. "After every life we live, we become stronger and truer, tempered by our experiences, until such time as we may complete our journey and we are truly born."[5]

Our soul needs to develop. It needs to learn compassion and unconditional love, and the best way to do that is to expand our love in an environment where there are many restrictions. If everything is perfect, then there are only a few opportunities to expand our ability to love. Therefore, restrictions are necessary. We need time restrictions, location restrictions, view restrictions, resource restrictions, and so on. This means living in our four-dimensional world, the world with less dimensions and less possibilities than the other part of our unity universe. We cannot learn everything in one lesson. We need many different experiences, and, therefore, repeated incarnations are required. This will help us to become our divine core. Only as a divine core can we finally approach the One who emits The Light.

NDErs often feel that there are many different levels in the unity universe. The more we are able to expand our love, the further we can proceed through all these levels. The final goal is to be close to The Light. As we know, The Light is extremely powerful and overwhelming, and to be able to approach It, we need to be similar. Because if we aren't, we would be blown apart. It would be our total destruction. For this reason, one NDEr feels that the light parts of our spirit would be able to proceed to higher levels, but that the denser or heavier parts would have to reincarnate again to have new opportunities to improve.

It is difficult or even impossible to establish whether these ideas are correct, but what is consistently repeated is that the array of experiences are there to foster love, and thereby to come closer to The Light. An example of how this is expressed can be found in the NDE account of Christian Andréason, a wonderful American recording artist and spiritual counselor.[6] On his Website, one can read:

"[I became] surrounded and observed by many beings and fellow Souls, who in reality (I somehow understood) had been standing near me during my entire lifetime! Every single one of these individuals was someone I knew very well, but did not recognize as having been a part of my life during this incarnation. Yet, the closeness and familiarity I felt for these beloved Souls surpassed any devotion for anyone I have ever learned to Love here on this planet. As I felt the energy and Love coming from these individuals, I knew that we were all family.

"Memories of past-life experiences with these beings filled my consciousness and as this happened I was filled with wonder at how truly eternal we all are!"

He then understands that life never ends, and that at the end of each lifetime, there will be a bridge to another lifetime. After seeing this sequence of lives, the scene changes and he moves away toward The Light. Again, he receives memories from former incarnations:

"...it struck me how all the moments (even those that might have seemed insignificant before) all turned out to be huge stepping stones when seen from an eternal perspective. I saw how even the most mundane or boring task had the ability to lead me to an even greater awareness about myself..."

He saw that there were many different experiences. In some lives he would be poor, in some wealthy, some were with beauty, others with disfigurement or disease. There was fame, misfortune, or a mixture of everything. He understands that this happens to everyone and that it is necessary to help us, "examine the unlimited amount of vantage points into the remarkable, endurable, unchangeable and complex natures of our own soul. To glimpse this (even once) in a single lifetime is truly a great blessing—as this is how we begin to truly recognize and define our own potential and behold our own wonder. All else is of the ego."

Apparently, we have to make a distinction between our own wonder on one hand, and ego on the other. We do this by advancing through many lifetimes in order to learn about love. This was also expressed by Christian Andréason in the opening quote of this chapter. That quote also reinforces the importance of being aligned with The Light.

Is reincarnation real?

There are NDErs who do not believe in reincarnation. They haven't seen it during their experience nor do they have the feeling that it is true. Betty Eadie, author of the best-seller *Embraced By the Light* says that our experiences are stored in our cells and are transmitted to our children.[7] If we seem to remember a previous life, we in fact have memories of others stored in our cells. This hypothesis, however, makes it difficult to explain how other NDErs say they can remember lives in many different countries, unless of course our ancestors traveled extensively.

There are some problems with the prevailing concept of reincarnation. Usually, we think of it as the transfer of our spirit into another body after the previous one has died. The assumption is that the spirit doesn't change; only the body does. It is a one-on-one move of the complete soul or spirit to the new body. In addition, people usually assume that we are reborn in the future, following the usual linear time pattern as we know it on earth. However, we already established that there is something strange going on with time. Time is not an issue when we die and arrive in the other part of the unity universe. The present blends with the future and the past. Therefore, it should also be possible to be born in a previous life, going backward in time. Nevertheless, people usually see past lives. They rarely see future lives.

When we discuss reincarnation, we should also remember that interconnectedness with everything is a central theme in NDEs. In this way, it is understandable that we feel connected with the single-celled organisms, because we have developed from them. The connection with other people in bygone times is also quite understandable when we take into account that all time exists all at once, and that we can have a simultaneous overview of the past and future. After all, we are in a unity universe and, in principle, we have access to every emotion and thought there ever was.

Consider this unity universe and then relate to one of the stories in the Upanishads, one of the important religious books of Hinduism. In Hinduism, it is believed that everyone has its own particle of the Supreme Spirit Brahman (who is the almighty God). In the Upanishads, a father tries to explain to his son how he has to interpret the equality between his own divine particle and the whole of the Supreme Spirit Brahman. The father asks his son to put salt in a bowl of water and to come back tomorrow. The salt, of course, dissolves in the water and makes every bit of it taste salty. He uses this example to show that the essence of God is everywhere and in everyone. The story of the father and the son ends here, but I'd like to extend it as follows.

The dissolved salt in the water represents The Light that is in all of us. Now suppose the bowl is very big; suppose it is the ocean, and we can draw many billions of cups of water from it.

Each cup represents a human who carries part of The Light, but who is separated from its source and from the other cups of water. When a human dies, his cup of water is tossed back into the ocean to be reunited with its source. When a baby is born, a new cup of water is drawn. The chance is extremely small that exactly the same salt molecules that had previously been thrown back into the ocean end up in this new cup. There are perhaps just a few of those molecules in the new cup and maybe this is sufficient to remember a previous life. In that case, we cannot speak about a full one-on-one reincarnation.

We may take this example a bit further. Maybe we don't even need one molecule to have memories of previous lives. It might be sufficient that the molecules of the new cup had contact with the molecules of the old cup at the time they were in the ocean together. All information may have been shared between all molecules; it becomes collective information. In this case, you enter into the field of a collective consciousness (maybe along the lines the psychiatrist and philosopher Jung described). My memories would then be partly or wholly accessible to you (and vice versa).

The truth surpasses everything

I don't mean to say that the example of the cups of water reflects the truth, or that one-on-one reincarnation does not exist. I merely want to demonstrate that reincarnation is easy to theorize about, but difficult to prove. Also, Christian agrees that the real truth about reincarnation far surpasses what we think reincarnation is, as do other NDErs who are sure about reincarnation. The truth about reincarnation can only be fully understood when we arrive in that other part of the unity universe. Therefore, talking about it while being restricted to our four-dimensional world is like an apple that pretends to know how it feels to be an orange.

CHAPTER 7

NEGATIVE DARKNESS EXISTS

"The power lies within your own mind, so create only good vibrations, at all times. Even when it seems dark, it is very important to create more light."
~MADGE SUMMERFIELD[1]

In the previous chapters, much has been said about how blissful and positive NDEs are, and that they carry wonderful messages for all of us. The most important one is that we shouldn't fear that we aren't loved, because we are. Moreover, we are not just loved, we are loved in an unimaginable way: It is completely unlimited and totally unconditional. The sphere in which this love can be felt seems to be the sphere where the beings of light can be found, and of course The Light itself.

Despite the many reports of blissful NDEs, there have also been reports of NDEs with many shades of negativity. Sometimes NDErs were allowed to see this negativity at a safe distance; sometimes there was a brief brush with it and its frightening effect was clearly felt. However, in a non-negligible number of cases, the NDE has been predominantly or completely fearful, terrifying, and even hellish. These I will call distressful NDEs. There is a feeling of terror and despair, which takes place in an environment with a complete lack of love, where The Light or other beings of light are absent. Like the blissful NDEs, these experiences felt very real indeed; they were described as more than real. Just as with blissful NDEs, the experiences were ineffable.

I refer to the environment or sphere where this negativity is felt as negative darkness. I explicitly call it negative darkness as opposed to positive darkness, because in some NDEs, people find themselves in a dark void that still feels very pleasant, peaceful, and loving.

Interestingly, negative darkness not only occurs during NDEs, but also afterward. Remember that NDErs keep an open door to the other part of the unity universe. This makes it possible for them to have contact with the sphere of light and sometimes even with The Light itself. In the same way, they have the ability to notice negative darkness, and are even occasionally confronted with it.

Although it is difficult to determine exactly what negative darkness is, what its origin is, or under what circumstances it occurs, it may be possible to say a little bit more about some of the causes of distressful NDEs. From some examples, we may even derive preliminary solutions as to how to escape negative darkness when we come into contact with it. However, I want to stress that no-one really knows why some people have a distressful NDE, nor why some have a positive one. Apart from the problem we have in defining bad and good, there is no way we can assert that distressful NDEs are there only for bad people, and blissful ones only for good people. Therefore, never judge anyone by their NDE. And certainly don't condemn anyone for a particular NDE, because condemnation is never really an act of love. If we do that, we are not at all in alignment with The Light. I stress this, because people condemn one another too easily. We should never judge anyone, except perhaps ourselves. That is something that emerges loud and clear from life reviews.

Negative darkness in NDEs

In blissful NDEs, experiencers cannot find words suitable enough to express the wonders of that other world. They speak about a colorful and brilliant world with magnificent trees, flowers, and, above all, the feelings of unlimited and unconditional love. In distressful NDEs, things are completely different.[2] The environment is dark, gloomy, bare, and repelling. Some describe it as hot, and some spot a burning fire, but most reports are that it is very cold. The reason for this cold is often said to be the absence of love. Some see a pit or a hole with mist, from which hands and arms are raised upward. It smells damp, like decay, and it is difficult to breathe.

Sometimes creatures are seen, some of which were previously seen in the tunnel. Some seem to be more human than spiritual. Occasionally, they are reported as trying to get into contact with living people, but the living cannot hear or see them. Other strange creatures are seen somewhere else during the NDE. Those creatures are also not real spirits. It is as if they neither belong to the spiritual, nor to the physical world. They are in limbo.

One NDEr said that they looked like deformed beings, with distorted, angry faces. They were angry and filled with hatred. "When we passed that dark area, it was as if the being of light that accompanied me aroused these creatures. It seemed as if they had been asleep. It could also be that they were in a kind of waiting room. When they noticed us, they raced toward me. At first it frightened me, but the being of light that was holding my hand told me not to be afraid and to look. Indeed, they came close, very close, but they couldn't touch me. I knew that if they wanted, they could come with us and be in the light. But they didn't want to. Or maybe they were not yet ready for it."

Another NDEr said that she realized that she was not alone. She saw millions of others who were continuously moving in the same way as if walking in circles.[3] Their being was between material and spiritual existence. They cannot go back to earth because they lack a body, but neither can they go ahead into the spiritual world.

Some people saw the devil or devil-like figures. Creatures were moaning, and they were desperate. They looked grey and gloomy. They were zombie-like people. Some looked only half human. Everyone seemed to be trapped in a most unfortunate state of existence. They were depressed and very sad. They looked washed out. It seemed that they were forever shuffling and moving around, not knowing where to go, who to follow, what to look for, or who they were. It seemed that they had to move forever. They seemed to be looking for something, but it was not clear what that was.

Communication seems to be completely different. In the heaven-like NDEs, it is easy, immediate, and always full of love and understanding. Here, there seems to be no constructive communication. There even seems to be no communication at all, causing people to feel completely alone. The total impression is one of isolation, loneliness, desolation, or even abandonment. Moreover, there is a feeling of rejection and hate, as well as a constant sense of danger and violence. There is much fear and panic. Some even felt the presence of an evil being.

In an extraordinary book on this subject, Howard Storm describes his distressful NDE, which he calls his fall into hell.[4] It is extraordinary because it is rare that someone dares to come out in the open and say that he has been in a hellish environment, and what has happened there. He describes himself as having been an avowed atheist, who was too preoccupied with building up his own ego to think about anyone else. He had no time for friends, thought compassion was for the weak, found most people to be a tiresome nuisance, hated the world, and had started to drink a lot of alcohol to try to be happy.[5]

In a hospital in Paris, he almost died from a punctured stomach. He became very confused after he left his body. He tried to communicate with his wife, who was sitting at the side of his hospital bed, but, of course, she didn't hear him. He was bewildered. He did not meet a nice loving light, but nice and friendly voices that lured him away from his bed. Since the experience was so very real, and because he was a confirmed atheist, he didn't think of the possibility of being in his afterlife. He thought he was hallucinating because of his illness, and was following doctors or nurses who would help him. After a while, the voices gradually became antagonistic and authoritarian. The sense of dread grew in him. When he suddenly realized he was in complete darkness, the insults started. Next, he was pushed around in the dark. The situation became ever more aggravating. He started to fight back. They started to bite and tear him, and seemed to have great fun. "They were playing with me just like a cat plays with a mouse."

He describes the creatures as "once human." They can be thought of as the worst imaginable persons stripped of every impulse of compassion. "Some of them seemed to be able to tell others what to do, but I had no sense of there being any organization to the mayhem. They didn't appear to be controlled or directed by anyone. Simply, they were a mob of beings totally driven by unbridled cruelty."

The description of his ordeal in his book is not complete. He didn't describe everything that had happened. He doesn't want to remember it anymore. "In fact, much that occurred was simply too gruesome and disturbing to recall. I've spent years trying to suppress a lot of it. After the experience, whenever I did remember those details, I would become traumatized." He also says that the experience was far worse than any nightmare, because it seemed more real than being awake. It was "super-real."[6]

Fortunately, there is a happy ending to this story. Based on this and some other accounts, I think there may be a general way out of hellish experiences (see page 134).

Darkness after NDEs

Even when people had a wonderful NDE, they are sometimes confronted with darkness after their experience. Betty Eadie writes how she had to be protected from demon-like creatures. Someone else felt blackness around her. She even heard the floor creak, and felt how the mattress of her bed moved as if someone was sitting on it. It was so clear, that even her husband, who did not have an NDE, had felt it. She suspects it to be her father, since he had died shortly before, and he had always had a very negative character. She didn't react with fright, but prayed a lot (The Lord's Prayer, because she is a Christian) and asked The Light from her NDE to help her earthly father.

Another example is from Desirée (see Chapter 5). For weeks after her NDE, she remained too open and vulnerable to the other part of the unity universe. Frequently, she would be floating in and out of her body, and at one time she found out that she really had great difficulty in reconnecting. She had felt how dark forces dripped from the walls. They tried to prevent her from repossessing her own body. They wanted to gain control of her heart so they could make it stop beating. They wanted her to die, and, therefore, to a large extent it resembles Betty Eadie's case.

She thought it was strange, because during her experience Christ had clearly told her to return and finish her tasks. He had told her to do certain things. If she died at that moment, she would not be able to do those things.

Fortunately, there was help. She saw angels hastening to assist her, but she also noticed that they were too weak to prevent the darkness from proceeding. It was too strong. Finally she asked, "God, please let me die now, or otherwise help me."

Immediately she got an order. "Look upon it! Because this is what you need for the rest of your life, to see how negativity works."

She says that it is difficult to describe the darkness that was attacking her. It shouldn't be pictured as horned creatures. It is more like "something" with a non-fulfilling feeling. It can be likened to the empty feeling she had felt during her out-of-body experiences when she was abused by her father. In any case, it is contrary to what the feeling was during her NDE. That had been truly fulfilling.

Reasons for negative darkness

One would think the message of NDErs is that everyone is loved and everyone is welcome, but what should we make of distressful NDEs? Their existence somehow seems to complicate things a bit. After all, it would have been easier when one could be sure that the other part of the unity universe only consists of a wonderful and heavenly place. Apparently, that is not the case.

Many suggestions have been given for the existence of distressful NDEs, but it should be stressed that nobody really knows the real reason.[7] At this time, I consider three broad explanations to be close to the truth.

The first explanation: randomness

Like it or not, there is a category of people who genuinely do not understand why they went through a distressful experience. They consider themselves average, non-perfect people, with no faults in particular that would make them deserve a distressful NDE. This would mean that they were randomly chosen to go through a distressful NDE.

Some of them found themselves to be in a dark void in which they didn't feel anything. This lasted for a considerable time. They knew they still existed, because they noticed they could think clearly, and were conscious of being there. For these reasons, I don't consider these experiences to be hallucinations, but real NDEs. Perhaps these people were parked there in a waiting mode, but we cannot be sure at all.

Others even saw frightening or non-understandable images, or felt the presence of evil or something dangerous. And just like with positive NDEs, it often takes years for these people to cope with their overwhelming experiences.

It has been suggested that some of these frightening experiences and hell-like visions may have been caused by a less-than-loving or fearful mindset just before "dying."[8] They may also be the result of a confrontation with one's own shadow,[9] those aspects of a person that were always repressed or denied.[10] In that sense, one could think that the distressful sides of the NDE are revealed for the healing and growth of the NDEr.

In any case, as long as we don't have more information, we should not rule out that some form of randomness might be involved. However, because The Light is almighty, and is capable of loving unconditionally in an unlimited way, I wish to believe that there is a purpose for these distressful NDEs, which we fail to see presently. After all, being restricted to our four dimensions, and having no clear access to the higher dimensions, we are very limited in what we know, and what we are capable of knowing.

The second explanation: turning away from The Light

This is not just one explanation, but a whole range, all boiling down to the same theme. The common theme is absence of The Light, which can be voluntary or involuntary, and, of course, all shades of grey in between.

People may still be too attached to earthly matters. This attachment may take many forms. An addiction causes attachment to, for instance, alcohol, drugs, sex, money, power, and so on.

The urge to exert influence on someone or something can also be a very powerful form of attachment. Some people just can't let go. In life they have had the feeling that the world cannot continue without their influence, or perhaps even their manipulation. When this trait has been strong enough, it may not just vanish at once at the moment of death. Attachment could also be caused by the urge to apologize for something the deceased did. This may well happen in cases of suicide.

In all these cases, there continues to be a full concentration on four-dimensional earthly matters. Consequently, one is not open to The Light that can only be experienced when one proceeds further beyond the four dimensions.

This attachment has also been likened to the ego fighting to remain in charge. The ego is rooted in fear and in the illusion that it is an independent entity that it has to preserve. This love of one's self is opposed to the situation in which we let go of our ego and subject ourselves to the more general love for everyone. In this way, hell in distressful NDEs may reflect the experience of an illusory, separative ego fighting a phantom battle.[11]

This all sounds moderate, but some NDErs put it in more extreme terms. People are free to choose, and when they consistently choose negativity during their lives, negative darkness may be their destiny afterward. Some are convinced that people go to hell when they do not believe in a higher power, and do not feel that they are personally accountable for their actions. While on earth, they have done what pleased them, without taking account of the feelings of others.[12]

Howard Storm, who wrote about his fall into hell, even goes so far as to state that people go there because they have sinned.[13] He defines sin as the denial of the existence of God, and the turning away from Him/Her. Sin is intentional separation from God, or however we want to call Him/Her. According to Storm, it is absolutely important that we conform ourselves to God. It is God's wish that we use our opportunities in life wisely and lovingly. When we fail to do that, we reject God. Separation from God is not something God wants. It is something people decide for themselves, of their own free will. Separation from God means that we are on our own, which means hell.

This seems a bit harsh, but something along the same lines (without that far-reaching implication) is said by other NDErs. If you look for love, you will get love; if you give love, you will receive it. But if you hate, or if you look for hatred, that is what you'll get. With respect to separation, some NDErs have a completely different idea. They are convinced that a full separation from The Light is utterly impossible, because we all are, and will always be, an indispensable part of it.

An example: suicide

One particularly important way we are able to voluntarily turn away from The Light is by committing suicide. Some people go as far as to say that suicide is a mortal sin. From the many testimonies, it seems that suicide is certainly not the best thing to do. These testimonies not only come from people who have actually tried to commit suicide, but also from people who have almost died as a consequence of a more natural cause. In general, all of them reject suicide as a possibility to go back to that wonderful other world. However, in a few cases, there have been suicide attempts for that purpose.

Monique Hennequin told me that her first NDE had all the standard characteristics.[14] It had been a wonderful experience, and she told The Light that she would go back to earth to accomplish a certain goal. When she became conscious in the hospital, she was almost completely paralyzed, and artificial respiration was applied to her through a tube in her mouth. She could only move her fingertips. She used them to signal to the nurses that she was conscious, but they thought that the movements were convulsions and injected her with muscle relaxant!

She realized that she would not be able to fulfill the task she had promised to The Light. Disappointed in The Light, and in her own situation, she decided to bite the tube through which she was artificially breathing and swallow it. In that way, she would be able to escape her situation and return to that wonderful Light. When she succeeded, and slipped out of her body again (into her near-death phase), she arrived in a "cold, nasty, black, rotten place." There, she also felt the presence of other souls that "had turned themselves away from God."

This was totally different from her previous NDE. She realized quickly that what she had done was not right, because she had given up courage and gratefulness. She was filled with remorse, and her intense remorse made her reconnect with love and compassion. This proved to be her rescue, because her deceased father came and made sure she could go back to her body. There, she found the nurses trying to apply artificial respiration to her with a hand-pump. Eventually, everything turned out all right, and now her body functions are well again. The experience made her see that her action to free herself from her body was not the best thing she could have done, and that she should have put a greater trust in The Light.

In another case, it was made absolutely clear that suicide is far from optimal. In this case, the person had a positive NDE after a motorcycle accident. Even though he didn't see The Light, he had an out-of-body experience, during which he had a peaceful feeling. Twenty years later, he was in the midst of many family troubles, and finally got divorced. It all took a big toll on him. One night he was drinking heavily, thought about his life, and how he had lost his family. Without hesitation, he put a gun to his head and pulled the trigger. "From that point, I had a visit from a lady; don't know who it was to this day. She was not from real life. She had told me I am not supposed to be there, that what I had done is very wrong, and that she was going to make it right again. Then I spent the next two weeks in a nightmare kind of state, living with awful things. Unlike the first time I died, she told me if I ever take my life again, this is what I would have to live with for eternity."[15]

What is remarkable is the regret that people have after attempting suicide, and their joy that it had failed. For them, suicide was clearly no longer an option. In addition, they were willing to counsel others against suicide.[16]

One person describes the effect of her attempted suicide as if she was throwing stones in a pond, creating ripples crossing over the entire world and changing it forever.[17] She saw how her selfish choice would hurt a lot of people, including those she would never meet. She saw how she would get stuck in the feeling of this destruction, and having wasted all the opportunities that life would hold to learn about love. That feeling was like a self-created hell.

At this point, I want to stress that not all people who made a failed suicide attempt have had a distressful NDE. There are some reports of blissful NDEs. Nevertheless, I have the strong feeling that if we want to avoid a hell-like environment, it is best not to commit suicide.

The third explanation: healing

Generally, distressful NDEs have the same after-effects as positive ones. They make people aware of the greatness of creation, that there is a reason for them being in it, and that they should add something positive to the world. In possibly all cases, people who have had a distressful NDE are encouraged to re-evaluate their life and make changes. It often comes as a relief, because it makes them aware that they not only should, but also can, change their lives, even when they previously thought it was impossible. The positive after-effects of distressful NDEs have been wonderfully described in Barbera Rommer's book *Blessing In Disguise*.[18]

An impressive example that I came across is from an NDEr I interviewed. This person was under a lot of psychological strain, because her marriage was on the brink of collapse. She said that she felt her world tumbling down around her as she lost her grip on her life.

One morning, after one of her many wakeful nights, she went to the living room and sat near the fireplace. Suddenly, she was sucked into a tunnel. Her speed increased immensely, there was nothing to hold onto. There was a lot of roaring in her ears. She saw nothing, and it was quite frightening. Finally, she arrived in a limitless space with black light.

She saw a huge black circle in this immense space. A little figure was sitting in the middle. She recognized herself. She saw herself from above, but, at the same time, she experienced sitting in the middle of that circle.

She had an intense feeling of loneliness, being lost and desolate. There was no one, no human, no movement, only blackness and a lot of emptiness.

Then something roared within her, "You love no one."

It crushed her. She knew, saw, and felt how she treated people. She understood that she had been living a lie. She had done a lot of things that other people would regard as "good," but she had done these things with the sole intention of benefitting from them herself, for her own self-interest, to be loved by others, and to be esteemed. She saw who she really was: a mask of compassion. It was horrible to see the truth.

The experience lasted less than five earthly minutes, but to her, it seemed to last a lifetime. Then, with a bang, she was back in her body, in the living room. She was devastated, in a state of total breakdown, and could do only one thing: cry.

It had been a very harsh wake-up call, but it woke her up for a second chance. It changed her completely. It was utterly difficult to cope with the experience, and at the same time, continue to look after her two young children. She found courage to look for a different way to live. She did it by herself, though there was also help from others. And she succeeded, because she firmly wanted to change.

Now she is absolutely convinced that intention is a key factor. Be true, look for truth, and don't live in pretense. Don't be a cheat and a liar. Do things with true loving intentions, because even when they fail, the good intentions will count. It is better to start with good intentions and do something that turns out wrong, rather than the other way around.

Even if we think we can keep our intentions and our deepest thoughts to ourselves, they are open and fully exposed in the other part of the unity universe. This is because the other part of us knows, and is in open connection with the rest of unity universe. So it is absolutely necessary to try to do everything with truly good intentions.

A second thing she is absolutely convinced of is that there is only love, and that we make our own punishment. A distressful NDE is not meant as a punishment, but it is an invitation to change and to come to your true self.

A way out?

The idea that we make our own punishment is an interesting notion. I do not know of one case in which The Light was annoyed, discontent, or even angry with someone. No one reported that The Light has looked up rules in the Bible, the Quran, the Bhagavad-Gita, the Torah, or any other important religious text, and confronted someone with them. Nor did It ever condemn anyone. On the contrary, also during the life review, when the NDEr gets deeper insights into his or her life, and sees where he or she could have chosen a more loving action, The Light and the beings of light continued to be full of understanding and compassion. Regularly, it has been said that they urged the NDEr not to be too harsh in judging him- or herself. Therefore, we should conclude that they are open to us, and it depends on us whether we are open to them.

In addition, remember what Tienke heard when she had an open connection with the realm of The Light. "Evil is nothing other than good that doesn't know itself." Evil people are still particles of The Light, albeit ones that cannot shine because they have been strangled or polluted. This means that when someone finally recognizes the good within, he or she will be able to turn to The Light and shine again.

All of this seems to be additional support for the second explanation mentioned before (note that the other two explanations still hold). It is us who turn away from The Light; we seem to punish ourselves. The Light doesn't punish. So, we shouldn't say that the terrible things that happen in our lives are punishments. Divorces, death of our loved ones, earthquakes, storms, unemployment, and also the current financial and economic crisis are not punishments. Neither is our life review, because if someone judges and seems to punish us, it is us. The Light remains unconditional and limitless in its love, and, therefore, a confrontation with negative darkness cannot be its punishment for us. This would imply that when we are confronted with negative darkness, the best thing to do is to turn to The Light for help. To direct ourselves toward It is to get aligned with It. And indeed, there is evidence that this works.

An NDEr found himself in the "biggest, largest, most vast pit of greyness that one could experience." He was shocked, not only because he felt it was terrible, but also because he instinctively knew that it was real. He decided to calm himself down, and with great effort, tried to do some meditation. While he was doing this, the place changed color. It went to a "rich, dark purple."

He stresses that the significance of the change of color wasn't merely visual. There was also a change in feeling. He said, "I felt as though a moment ago I'd been faced with someone holding a gun barrel to my head. When the color changed, it was as though he then said, 'Ok, we are not really interested in you,' and took the gun away."[19]

His feeling of sheer terror then subsided. He allowed himself to think, "Maybe this won't be so bad."

By meditating, he made his emotions neutral, and he moved from a negative into a neutral environment, where there was no hell, but also no Light. There are many more examples in which NDEs started off badly, but turned out well. I believe that we are able to divert ourselves away from the hellish environment, and to direct ourselves into The Light. When we are there, we are safe.

From reports of other NDErs, it appears that people who are trapped in a hell-like environment, are not left to fend for themselves.[20] This also applies to people who seem to wander around the earth after their death, because of their attachment to physical matters, such as their material possessions, or an alcohol or drug addiction; who wander around because they are still thoroughly occupied with influencing surviving relatives and friends; who undergo the consequences of their suicide over and over again. In all those cases, there are beings of light in their immediate vicinity, ready to lend a helping hand. This potential help can only be seen when the unfortunate NDErs decide to open their spiritual eyes, tap their spiritual core, and return to the light within them. This is easier when they have practiced love while on earth. The only requirement is that they themselves ask for help and accept the help that is offered. This, in turn, requires that these people become conscious of their loveless actions and feel remorse.

This was also the case with Howard Storm.[21] While his tormentors were swarming around him, he heard a voice (which sounded like his own) saying that he should pray to God. At first, he thought it was a stupid idea, but after he heard the voice a few more times, he tried. He murmured some churchly sounding phrases, and even the line with reference to God from The Pledge of Allegiance. This made the demons go mad, but they retreated nevertheless.

Because he cited the phrases without real affection, the retreat of the gruesome creatures was all he could realize. Although he felt they remained near, he was alone. However, there was also no heavenly Light, either. After he thought for a while about his miserable situation and about his egoistic life, which he started to regret, he made a genuine effort to pray. He prayed to Jesus, because that was the first person who came into his mind. After all, he was brought up as a Christian. Then, far off in the darkness, he saw a pinpoint of light rapidly coming closer. When it was near, he saw that it was the one he had been calling for, Jesus, who finally brought him out of his miserable position into The Light.

"Hatred does not cease by hatred, but only by love; this is the eternal rule."

~Buddha

"Negative darkness does not cease by our fear, but only by our desire to love (or our focus on love)."

~(Robert) Christophor Coppes

CHAPTER 8

GREAT CHANGES

"What you think matters; in fact, it forms matter."
~Varja Ghanta Gadan (1991)

Several NDErs are convinced that our world is going through a much-needed major change. For instance, in his book about his distressful NDE, Howard Storm writes that this major change is a spiritual revolution that will affect every person in the world.[1]

Another NDEr told me she had seen that the sun suddenly revolved more quickly. This didn't mean that it would literally be revolving more quickly, but she understood that we are going to make a major turn, and see an important transformation. According to her, this is unavoidable. We all have to go through it.

And finally, I should mention an interesting message from an NDEr who I interviewed in March 2008, and who correctly foretold the aggravation in September 2008 of the worst financial and economic crisis since the Great Depression of the 1930s, which is nowadays referred to as the Great Recession. These three NDErs are not alone. Many more express their feeling that things need to change because the way we treat each other and nature is unsustainable. Some are pessimistic about the developments, but this might be because at first we will go through a great deal of pain. Others are definitely optimistic, and express their firm belief that mankind will eventually change, and it will be for the better. Much better times seem to be in store for us.

Apparently, these are crucial times. We seem to have arrived at a crossroad. One NDEr said, "At the moment, humanity is going through the struggles of its adolescence. Who am I now? Who do I want to be? Will we choose for our soul or for our ego?"

He added, however, that he thought it would be exciting to see what role negative darkness plays.

Choosing which way to go is difficult, because we don't have an overview of what is happening. What is going on? What are we about to discover? Where do we need to go from here?

The confusing landscape we are in is partly caused by the Great Recession, which has given many of us an acute feeling of pain. The other part of the confusion may be less acute, but nonetheless, poses a serious threat to mankind. It is the way we treat nature.

What can we learn from NDErs about our current situation and how can we smoothly bring about this much-needed change?

Birth pains

At first, we have to recognize that we are more than just a material body that easily learns to enjoy material things. We must realize that, beside this material aspect, we are a spiritual being too, and that this spiritual part of us is eternal. It is part of something so much greater, which I called the unity universe. One consequence of being part of the unity universe is that we all are interconnected in a spiritual, as well as material, way. Everything we do and think has an effect on the visible and invisible world around us. It ripples beyond our own immediate surroundings, and affects other people throughout the world. Likewise, acts of other people also have an effect on us, even when we don't know them.

It is very understandable that we have forgotten about our spiritual part, because the four-dimensional material world is very obtrusive. Its very clear presence overshadows the more subtle spiritual world. However, this spiritual world is really there. We know about it through NDEs. And through them, we also know about our interconnectedness. What we have seen happening with the Great Recession is the effect of the tidal wave of negative ripples that we created together, and that backfired on us due to this interconnectedness. Therefore, it's about time that we concentrate less on our financial wealth, and pay more attention to our spiritual wealth.

In these times we are discovering that it is beneficial for us not to go against the nature of The Light, but, instead, become aligned with It. Remember that its nature is unconditional, limitless love. Because we are part of this Light, we could know about this unconditional love. It is already somewhere within us. We just have to learn to feel It and to express It. This means that, at least, we need to have a greater respect for all there is, that is, for other people, for animals, and in fact, for all nature. I say "at least," because respect is the first stage of unconditional, limitless love. To put it differently, respect is a derivative of this pure form of love. An important aspect of respect is honesty and integrity. The lack of these two has created this economic and environmental mess we have run into.

The NDEr who correctly foretold the Great Recession compared this painful transition we are going through to birth pains. The pain may truly be considerable, but we cannot avoid it. Like a future mother in labor, we should also be thrilled that we are present to experience this great and beneficial change. In fact, we all are courageous, because all of us have voluntarily chosen to play our part on earth at this crucial and difficult time. She allowed me to write about her preview of the economic crisis under the condition that I would also write that we will eventually come through this painful transition, and that we are destined to head for a more wonderful world, materially, as well as spiritually. Apparently, more of us will get aligned with The Light.

The Great Recession or the Great Implosion

Currently, we are still struggling with the aftermath of the worst financial and economic crisis since the Great Depression of the 1930s. It is the most severe economic crisis in living memory, and we are still licking our wounds. Sometimes it is referred to as the Great Recession, but because it was the result of the virtual collapse of the financial system, with the bankruptcy and near-bankruptcy of major financial institutions, it may seem more appropriate to refer to it as the Great Implosion.[2]

When the Great Recession was only in its first phase, I had one of my interviews with an NDEr. The crisis had started in August 2007, and lingered on until Bear Stearns, one of the major investment banks, was running into serious problems. I spoke with her in March 2008, right after Bear Stearns had been saved by JP Morgan/Chase in a deal brokered by the Federal Reserve. Everyone was sighing with relief and stock prices quickly recovered from their previous losses. Due to excess world demand prices of oil, other commodities, as well as food, were heading north. Oil still had to reach its all-time high of almost $150 per barrel in the summer of that year.

While people out there were scrambling to buy stocks again, she told me that this episode with Bear Stearns was just the beginning. She said, "What is happening in America is just the forerunner of the real crisis. The real crisis is still to come, and it will really be severe. Many people will be affected, including my family. One of my children will be drawn into this… Everything that is detrimental to human beings is wrong, be it economical or environmental. Materially, a new world is being created. Also, people who misuse the earth will be confronted with results of their own wrongdoing."

She had been given this information in her NDE in 1986, but she didn't understand it because it came in this elevated form of communication. The knowledge became intangible after her experience. In addition, she is not knowledgeable about finance, and for that reason alone, she was not able to explain what she had seen. However, the turmoil that started in 2007, which led to the fearful tension preceding the Bear Sterns rescue, made her understand that this was the time-frame that she had seen in 1986. Her feelings during the NDE matched the fearful tension she sensed in the world of March 2008.

I didn't really give much thought to it. I made my notes and went on with my life until September of that year. The two gigantic mortgage banks, Fannie Mae and Freddie Mac, and the biggest insurance company in the world, AIG, ran into mounting problems. Until that moment, the failure of these three mammoth financial firms had not been thought possible. Finally, they had to be saved by the U.S. Treasury. In fact, they were all nationalized: the two agencies entirely and the insurer effectively for about 80 percent. Then, in mid-September 2008, Lehman Brothers, another investment bank, went belly-up and this triggered the gradual break down of the financial system as we had known it since World War II. It led to the full or partial nationalization of many more banks and insurance companies in Europe and the United States. The breakdown of the financial system caused the most severe economic crisis the world had experienced since the Great Depression of the 1930s and made central banks around the world resort to what has become known as "unconventional policy measures."

She had been right all along.

She and the other NDErs knew that we have to go through this situation. It is unavoidable. We need to learn from it, and we must change ourselves. We all have to turn around. What we have done up to now, and how we lived, is unsustainable.

Another NDEr told me that she too had seen that all of this was going to occur. In October 2007, she sold all her equity before the stock markets everywhere in the world plunged by more than 50 percent at the end of 2008. This is a unique case of "insider trading."

Dishonesty

Let's take a look at what happened and then see what NDErs have to say about it.

The housing boom in the United States started with the policy of low-interest rates that the Federal Reserve thought necessary to accommodate the effects of a previous crisis: the bursting of the dot-com bubble in 2000. Therefore, the Fed is often blamed for indirectly causing the current crisis, but I will argue that we ourselves are to blame for it. In any case, the low interest rates led to an unprecedented boom in the housing market. More and more houses were sold, and prices were skyrocketing. Mortgages became a booming business; the market proved to be very profitable for banks, mortgage brokers, and many others.

After a while, the number of people who could afford houses at these elevated prices decreased. The business had to think of something to keep everyone going. Ingenious mortgage constructions were invented and sold to people who could otherwise not afford houses at these high prices. This was done, for instance, with teaser rates, where one could start with a ridiculously low interest rate, but after a few years, the interest rate would be adjusted upward. They went sky-high to more than compensate for the low starting rates. In most cases, the homeowners didn't know about this increase, or didn't understand it. Needless to say, they were not able to pay the increase. However, the involved bank employees and brokers knew in advance that this would be the case, but they were primarily interested in a high, short-term mortgage production.

Sustaining the turnover of mortgages was also achieved by telling people when they were filling out their mortgage applications that they could lie about their income or home situation. These were the so-called liar loans. People were misled in many different ways to borrow way beyond their capacity.

All of this cheating and deceiving has become known as predatory loan practices: making profits at the cost of others. This kind of profit-making is fundamentally an antisocial behavior. Instead of a win-win situation, the mortgage business became an I-win-you-lose market creating so-called sub-prime mortgages. Short-term self-interest of all who were involved in expanding the sub-prime mortgage market caused all of this. These practices did not only occur in the housing business, but in other businesses as well.

There was an abundance of financial constructions, but at the same time a great lack of integrity. On one hand, there were the mortgage-sellers who knew they were selling loans that homeowners were never going to be able to repay. Their intentions were dishonest. Their actions had nothing to do with integrity or respect for others, let alone with love. On the other hand there were the people who took out mortgages on houses they couldn't afford. They often didn't know that they were digging their own financial grave.

This was not all. Securities firms mixed the mortgages and repackaged them. The new securities that came out of this process were sold in the capital markets. To make them appetizing, they were rated by specialized agencies. However, there are only a few of these rating agencies, and they were having increasing problems grasping the ingenious, but complex, details of these new securities. Consequently, it became more and more difficult for them to come up with sound ratings.

Money provided an efficient smoothing factor, because the rating agencies were handsomely paid for their ratings. And guess who was paying. The securities firms were! This situation can be compared to the poacher paying the salary of the gamekeeper. Apparently, the rating agencies were not free to assign ratings, but they didn't really mind. They fell for the seductive power of money, paid for by the securities firms who needed high ratings to market their products. After all, a fancy name for the securities is a good start, but it doesn't do the trick all by itself.

It was established from e-mails released after a Congressional investigation that employees of rating agencies privately had their doubts about the soundness of their ratings. One said that they had created a monster. Two other quotes are, "Let's hope that we are all wealthy and retired by the time this house of cards falters" and "…these errors make us look either incompetent at credit analysis or like we sold our souls to the devil for revenue." And a final quote to show that they would do anything to rate any financial construction, "It could be structured by cows and we would rate it."

They too had dishonest intentions, because they knew, but told no one in order not to jeopardize their own material position: the profit of the agency, their own bonuses, their jobs and wages, and their pension scheme. This is extreme self-interest at work. There was no respect for the well-being of others. There was no integrity. There was no supervision, no checks and balances.

In itself, the business of repackaging, or the securitizing of, for instance, mortgages is not bad at all; it can be very beneficial to society as a whole because it can enhance wealth. But the repackaging of crap and selling it as if it was gilt-edged is cheating; it is devious. This and other sorts of repackaged "crap debt" have become known as toxic debt.

Occasionally, even people who were behind the wheel acknowledged the dishonest practices of financial institutions. For example Henry Kaufman, who served in top management positions with the investment bank Salomon Brothers, indicated that financial institutions were in distress because they cultivated dishonesty.[3] It is interesting to hear this from his mouth knowing that he had been one of the executive directors at Lehman Brothers, right at the time when the firm went bust. He had been responsible for the Finance and Risk Committee.

Apparently, banks themselves didn't have sufficient mechanisms in place to counter these dishonest lending practices that have euphemistically become known as "irresponsible lending practices." Even Greenspan, head of the Federal Reserve during the real estate boom, and firm believer in the capitalist market economy, had to admit this. He was "shocked," as he put it, that the self-interest of organizations did not lead to adequate surveillance of their own activities, or to sufficient self-regulation. Of course it didn't work. What else can you expect when banks are run by individuals who only know to act based on their own self-interest (their bonuses, for instance), and are not interested in their clients any more. Mr. Greenspan (and others) must wake up to the idea that pure self-interest is a very shallow concept.

The cost

And what did all of this cost us? The sub-prime mortgages, the trigger of the Great Recession, caused banks to write-down many hundreds of billions of dollars. In turn, this led to further losses on other financial products, and finally to a gradual crash of the stock markets. The Bank of England estimated that the worldwide total of write-downs on the market value of financial instruments, including the toxic assets, would amount to a whopping $2.8 trillion at the end of October 2008. In 2010, the International Monetary Fund published its own estimation of around $2.3 trillion. If you add the losses on all the stock markets in the world in 2008, the figure becomes even more astronomical—a staggering $26 trillion.

These losses are unprecedented. During peacetime, there has never been any greater destruction of wealth than during this crisis. This amount of value destruction is truly unimaginable.

Therefore, relate these amounts to something else. Everyone in the United States, including companies and the government, would have to work for approximately two full years, devoting all of that money to the debt, to produce $26 trillion. Now take a look at the smaller amount of $2.8 trillion of direct losses. Everyone in the United Kingdom has to work one full year to get that amount together. In South America, the annual production of all countries combined just falls short of $2.8 trillion.

The amount of money the U.S. government spends annually on Medicaid, Medicare, and the State Children's Health Insurance Program is only about one fifth of the $2.8 trillion. Compared to this loss, the amount needed to halt the AIDS-epidemic in developing nations will almost sound like a giveaway. Stopping AIDS and all the misery that comes with it (such as babies and children that see both parents die and are left alone to care for themselves) only costs approximately $20 billion, which is less than 1 percent of this $2.8 trillion.[4] And finally, compared to the financial losses, the total funds available for malaria control in all of Africa seem like peanuts: a mere $700 million.

The root cause: excessive short-term self-interest

For many decades, we have learned to pursue our own self-interest, and we were taught that this is honorable. Economic theory says so, and after communism collapsed in 1989, capitalism is the only economic guide around. It is based on the idea that the pursuit of individual self-interest unintentionally leads to the biggest product for society as a whole, and everyone would be better off. This happens through a kind of "invisible hand."

This idea of an invisible hand was introduced by the god-father of capitalism, economist Adam Smith in his famous book *The Wealth of Nations*, published in 1776. People who almost religiously believe in the infallibility of self-interest often quote the following passage from his book, "It is not from the benevolence of the butcher, the brewer, or the baker that we expect our dinner, but from their regard to their own interest. We address ourselves not to their humanity, but to their self-love, and never talk to them of our own necessities, but of their advantage."

Self-interest requires individuals and companies to maximize their own profits. This would eventually lead to the maximization of total consumption in society. This theory has made us think of our own position first, and disregard that of others, although that extreme position was not what Adam Smith advocated. It is less well-known that Smith valued the importance of prudence, humanity, justice, generosity, and public spirit.[5]

Along the way, in our excessive pursuit of self-interest, we learned not to care about others. We wanted to have more for ourselves, and having enough was not sufficient. Greed kicked in. Money was no longer the energy to achieve something productive, something creative, or something that would add to our world in a positive way. We were not aiming for a win-win situation for us and for the others with whom we dealt. As one

NDEr said, "Money became the goal itself and not anymore a means. Our world is based on money and everything else is made subordinate to it." We go for the money, even if it means a loss-situation for the other. This is greed. By acting this way, we showed no respect for others.

We didn't care about them. We were indifferent to their suffering. Through our greed and indifference, we created an I-don't-care-about-you-society. And this has brought us this current crisis. One NDEr explicitly told me that, "The crisis is based on the combination of greed and indifference. However, you can't be indifferent; you have to care!"

A young man, who had his NDE due to a severe kidney problem when he was eight, said something along the same lines. His NDE was quite complete, with many of the standard features, such as a tunnel, a bright light, a vision of a paradise-like environment, a life-review, and the feeling of unconditional love, peace, and acceptance. His deceased grandfather accompanied him during his experience, and also showed him the future.

"Now I see and experience things that I already saw 21 years ago. I find this surreal, very difficult to comprehend. I saw the earth from above, hovered through time and space of the universe and saw everything. Humanity is caught up in an emotional obsession for money. Wanting more and more while real riches can be found within ourselves. We are now in an economic crisis and everyone is thrown into confusion of how to get back the old economy, but one will see that this is not possible. We are entering a period of time which is meant to make us understand that happiness is to be found in other things."

Although there are good signs of economic recovery, we are not completely out of the woods yet. Moreover, at this moment we know for sure that famous financial institutions have left the stage or had a "Near-Death Experience," and the whole banking sector has changed beyond recognition. Major industrial giants have gone through bankruptcy proceedings, such as GM and Chrysler, and so did entire countries, such Iceland and, in fact, also Dubai. Along the way, the Great Recession drew heavily on public finances, which are in disarray in many countries. Greece became the first Western country that entered the danger zone because of this, and there are others lining up. Some economists even whisper that the United States and the United Kingdom might, at some time, be in such great financial difficulties that they are left with no other choice than to default on their debt. In any case, one can safely predict that the aftermath of the Great Recession will be felt for quite a while and that a full recovery will definitely take a great deal of time.

In addition, there is still the danger of a relapse, something that happened several times in the 1930s. If we don't fundamentally change, we will have these relapses, and we will see more crises. Actually, the NDEr who mentioned the combination of greed and indifference said something similar. She said, "If we return to business as usual, the whole thing will happen again in some or other form. And the next crisis will occur closer to this one. It will be more like instant karma: you do something, and immediately you'll get slapped in the face."

Other NDErs are sure that there is still more to come. According to one of them, "the worst is yet to come. There is a great inequality in wealth. We are living 'Marie Antoinette times' all over again."

He referred to queen Marie Antoinette who was married to Louis XVI, the last king of France. The French Revolution toppled their thrones, and they were both beheaded. According to the story, Marie Antoinette was told that the people were suffering from famine, and had no bread to eat. She allegedly responded, "Let them eat brioche (a kind of cake)." Although most probably a previous French princess said this, the quote was later used to demonstrate the complete ignorance and extreme self-interest of the excessively rich French royals and nobles, and the church in those days. The NDEer explained that we see something similar today, where the people at the top have lost all sense of reality while being consumed with greed. He hopes that the eventual reversal of this excessive inequality doesn't give rise to a contemporary Napoleon of some sort.

Manhandling of nature

Whereas the focus has been on the economy (and as an economist this topic is close to my heart), one NDEr told me not to focus on the credit crisis alone. "The credit crisis is really just the tip of the iceberg. Our greed is bringing disorder to the whole system of earth."

When asked about nature, another NDEr said, "The feeling I have is terrible. What we do to earth is incredible. It cannot continue like that."

The young man with the kidney condition whose grandfather showed him the future said, "I understood that *we* are nature, and that it is urgently needed to change our behavior. Otherwise, we will destroy the whole lot: nature, the earth, and therefore also mankind." This coincides very well with the idea of a unity universe: In the end, everything belongs to one great whole, where The Light is the binding factor: I am you, you are me, we are nature, nature is us.

Some other NDErs have said things such as, "There will be more natural disasters," and, "There are some climate processes, which cannot be stopped anymore. We are on the eve of great disasters. It has to do with water, but that seems a bit obvious now."

Obvious or not, problems with water have been a recurring theme in NDEs. For instance, at an IANDS conference, someone told me that in his NDE, he had seen three things that were going to take place. These were the collapse of some important tall buildings that would shock the world, a destructive flood that would affect many people along endless stretches of coastlines, and something that resembled people being pulled back from the ocean shores. The first event he recognized when 9/11 occurred, and the second when the Christmas tsunami of 2004 struck. The third event has yet to take place.

The NDEr who correctly predicted the Great Recession in March 2008 was also sure something was going to happen, and that it has to do with water. However, she was not able to explain exactly what it was. During the NDE, it is perfectly clear what is meant, but once back in the four space-time dimensions, the knowledge can no longer be accessed. As with the credit crisis, she will possibly remember it again when something happens that would fall into place with the feelings she had during her NDE. She said she is not afraid of what might come, but, nevertheless, decided to buy an inflatable boat and store it in her garage.

It is perfectly normal that we use nature and its resources to sustain ourselves, and even to increase our standard of living. We have been doing that throughout history. But until the industrial revolution, mankind had a negligible effect on nature. That changed. Our influence on nature was stepped-up after the start of the industrial revolution. The scale on which we currently influence nature has increased in such a way that we can feel its effect everywhere, and it starts to threaten mankind itself.

One example that needs no further explanation is the great oil spill in the Gulf of Mexico, which started in April 2010, and lasted for several months. It has caused immeasurable damage. But I could also mention the extinction and near-extinction of many forms of vegetation and animal species. One NDEr was shocked by the little compassion there is with, for instance, the bluefin tuna. Even though this particular tuna is almost extinct, there is still a great demand for its meat, and it was impossible to reach an international agreement to prevent full extinction. The consequence: In a few years, there will not be bluefin tuna sushi on our menus.

The Eastern and Western Rubbish Patches in the Pacific Ocean are prime examples of pollution. These immense garbage dumps are formed from the plastic junk we continuously toss into the ocean. Anything made of plastic you can think of is there, such as Lego blocks, footballs, bottles, fishing nets, pacifiers, and all sorts of wrappings. These garbage dumps are unimaginably large. Although the exact size is yet unknown, some scientists estimate these patches to be twice the size of the United States. They are not solid islands, but more like a soup of plastic that is held in place by swirling underwater currents. Plastic doesn't decay; however, under the influence of sunlight, and the continuous wash of seawater, it degrades into ever-smaller particles. This is how the plastic soup is brewed: We provide the ingredients, while nature does the rest. The soup is consumed by aquatic organisms and animals, and thus enters the food chain (including ours). It not only threatens the health of marine animals and birds, but our own as well.

Apart from the plastic soup, there is much more on our menu. The main course would still be air pollution, which is causing global warming. The Organization for Economic Co-operation and Development in Paris estimates that if we continue with "business as usual," the global temperature will increase in the coming decades by 3 to 4 degrees Fahrenheit.[6] It may not seem like much when we look at our thermostat, but outside our homes it definitely is.

In March 2009, in Copenhagen, Denmark, there was a conference at which the world's top climate scientists discussed the latest findings in their fields.[7] The conclusions of this scientific conference are really alarming. The first conclusion was that the observed emissions of carbon dioxide are so high that previously thought of worst-case trajectories will actually be realized. For many key parameters, the climate system is already moving beyond known boundaries. These include mean surface temperature, sea-level rise, ocean and ice sheet dynamics, ocean acidification, and extreme climate events. Moreover, there is a significant risk that many of the trends will accelerate, leading to an increasing risk of abrupt or irreversible climate shifts.

Further conclusions are that our societies are highly vulnerable to even modest levels of climate change. Poor nations are particularly at risk. Temperature rises of more than 4 degrees Fahrenheit will already be very difficult to cope with. Scientists consider 4 degrees unavoidable as things develop now. However, there are some scientists who have calculated temperature rises of up to 11 degrees Fahrenheit. That would really be disastrous!

Global warming will make our oceans a bit warmer, which will cause more hurricanes to ravage cities near our shores. We are already experiencing this. It will also cause more rainy days, and the rain will not be spread evenly over the surface of our planet. Some places will see much heavier rains and, consequently, more damaging floods and mud slides. But in other places, there will be increased heat waves and intense draughts.

There will be more deserts. The climate change will differ between countries and regions, and have different effects on us and future generations.

According to some ecologists, the credit crisis will be nothing compared to the environmental problems we will encounter. This coincides with what an NDEr said about the tip of the iceberg. The Copenhagen conference concludes that there is no excuse for inaction. We already have many tools and approaches to effectively deal with the challenge of climate change. We have the economic means, technological know-how, and managerial knowledge, but they must be vigorously and widely implemented to achieve the required transformation of our society and create decarbonized economies. We just have to decisively direct our energy and resources at that goal, and it will come about.

It will have great benefits too! There will be a sustainable energy job growth, reductions in health and economic costs (because, if we do nothing, these will be huge), and the restoration of ecosystems.

Apart from a global rise in temperature, there is another serious and partly related problem: the shortage of water for an increasing world population. In all but a few places worldwide, clean water is becoming increasingly scarce, even in the United States, with Las Vegas as an excellent example. Las Vegas uses more water than there is supply from the Colorado River, which feeds Lake Mead. If nothing changes, the lake could run dry in 2021. In fact, the city uses more water than there is supply. Currently, it is a known problem, and in television programs,

we are informed about it. However, NDErs have been expressing their concern for many decades.

For example, one NDEr told me that from her NDE,
which took place 30 years ago, she knew that the distribution
of water would become a serious problem. According to her,
fights and possibly even battles will occur over water. However,
only recently, there are scientists who predict that the climate
change will lead to wars. But it's not only the lack of clean drinking water that does it. The worldwide rise in temperature also
threatens food production, especially in poor countries. People
will try to migrate to places where there is food and water,
and this migration will lead to conflicts. Actually, the desperate
situation in Darfur, Sudan, is regarded as the first climate war.
The desertification boosted the struggle between communities
in that country. There will be more of these Darfur-kind of
internal conflicts, but we cannot rule out that there will also be
full-blown, cross-border wars and increased terrorism.

According to many NDErs, the environmental challenge is
a very important topic, but expanding more on this falls outside the scope of this book. Nevertheless, the message is that
NDErs have been warning us already for a long time about the
way we treat our environment, and that severe problems lay
ahead if we don't change quickly.

CHAPTER 9

THE SOLUTION:
GET ALIGNED WITH
THE LIGHT

"I want to go with the universal flow. I want my free will to be in accord with universe. I don't want it to be in the way of my fulfillment."
~ANONYMOUS NDER[1]

Our extreme self-interest in economic matters and in the way we treat nature made us dishonest, and caused us to have negative intentions. This created a whole host of negative ripples that were bound to come back to us in one form or another. This may seem depressing, but it shouldn't be. It's true that crises are stressful. Think of any crisis in your own life, and you'll agree. But crises also give us choices. They bring new opportunities to change, to correct what was wrong, and importantly, to move on in a more optimal direction. That applies to individuals, but also to humanity as a whole. And the current crisis is no exception. It will eventually have a very beneficial effect on us, because it will correct the excessive selfishness, and make us more aware of our dual nature.

We have to be glad that this is happening, because what we are experiencing, and what is yet to come, is a wake up call. We have to listen to it. It is, so to speak, a "kick in the butt" as was mentioned in Chapter 5. It is absolutely necessary that we become conscious of our interconnectedness and the ripple effect in the unity universe.

When we are aware that we can create ripples, the important question becomes: What can we do to create the positive ones that are beneficial to us and to everyone else? The answer will be surprisingly easy.

What are we about to discover?

The worst financial crisis in living memory reminds us that we are part of the unity universe in which we are all profoundly interconnected. Our interconnectedness makes everything we do have an effect somewhere else. All our actions, even the seemingly insignificant ones, ripple through this universe. The details of the transmission mechanism may yet be unknown, but the transmission is there, and should definitely not be ignored. There are interesting theories about how this transmission works. For example, Ervin László, the Hungarian philosopher of science, member of the Club of Rome, and founder of the Club of Budapest, introduced the Akashic Field Theory while NDE researcher Pim van Lommel assumes the existence of non-local consciousness.[2]

Whatever theory you want to think of, NDErs are absolutely certain that being part of this unity universe makes all of us interconnected. Interconnectedness is a recurring theme in NDEs. Therefore, focusing on pure self-interest is being terribly short-sighted. We shouldn't think that we are more important than others. Neither should we think that we are inferior to anyone else, because each of us has the ripple-creating power that lies within our own minds. It is our inner Light that is capable of creating ripples and having effect on others. If we willingly cheat someone else, we create negative ripples. And when this someone realizes the effect of our cheating, his or her emotional pain will also cause negative ripples. All these ripples travel somewhere through unity universe; they can't just disappear unnoticed.

This was nicely put into words by one NDEr. "Everything I do has influence on everything. Nothing is lost. It is a kind of law of conservation of energy. That is why we shouldn't do to others what we don't want for ourselves. Moreover, what we send, we'll attract. We should also be mindful of our thoughts, because we create with our thoughts."

An important part of what we have to discover is that each and every one of us has the ripple-creating power. We cannot hide behind the idea that we are small, weak, or insignificant. We don't have to be a president, prime minister, CEO, or head of a department to make a difference. We are individually responsible for our own ripples and the energy that it creates. Therefore, we all have to create positive ripples, and try to stop the negative ones. A graphic example of creating a negative ripple and stopping it immediately is what happened during the 2008 campaign for the U.S. presidential elections.

Many people were made to believe President Obama is a Muslim. The purpose of this obvious lie was to frighten them by associating him with terrorists. Those who started this lie had the dishonest intention to distort the truth in order to influence the outcome of the elections. In fact, this is similar to selling mortgages to people who cannot afford them, and by now we should know what dishonesty can lead to. And besides, what is wrong with being a Muslim? The Light unconditionally loves everyone, and it may startle some people, but this includes even Muslims.

There are too many examples in history where people were made to believe that a certain group is malicious. This creates extremely negative ripples. If enough people create these negative ripples, the outcome is devastating, as was sufficiently demonstrated by the witch hunts in medieval times, and more recently, the extermination camps of the Nazi regime in Europe. Fortunately, John McCain courageously spoke in the defense of Barack Obama, and stopped the negative ripple in its track.

Here is another example of stopping negative ripples. One of the reasons why World War I finally ended was because men from the German navy refused to go to battle any longer to fight the endless and useless war for their emperor. In the naval port of Kiel, they deserted and went ashore where they were accompanied by other German soldiers. Together, they marched on Berlin. It happened, even though it was in the final stages of the war. The war-loving German emperor had to flee to Holland, where he was given asylum.

We have to understand that we all have influence over the outcome, and we always have. We are responsible for what we create with our ripples. In addition, we must realize that we are able to neutralize negative ripples. The power lies within our own minds, so it would be good to consciously and continuously create positive ripples and send out good vibrations. It is very important that each and every one of us does that, even when we feel small and insignificant. We have to consciously create more light and more positive ripples, especially when it seems dark.

Through the financial and environmental crises, we will become more conscious of our own mind power. In the end, we will come through this turmoil wiser and better. Unfortunately, not everybody will choose this course, but a sufficiently great number of people will. These are the birth pains of what ultimately will be a miraculous, wonderful new world. We will all benefit from it, but now it is the time to endure, and the time to remain courageous.

Where do we need to go from here?

There are four steps we can take. It would be really nice to follow them as one, because then we would definitely feel our interconnectedness, but in any case, it is important that we do this individually. Remember, each of us has influence on the unity universe.

First, we should become conscious of our dual nature. From NDEs, it becomes clear that we don't only have a material body, but more importantly, we have a spiritual body or soul, which is an indispensable and eternal part of the unity universe. Because we are part of the unity universe, we also have effect on it. This takes place through the power of our minds. We must not underestimate this power. It is so powerful that it causes ripples, which will be felt elsewhere in the unity universe, including our four dimensional world.

Secondly, we need to realize that, to a large extent, we are free to choose, and we have to become conscious of our choices. We used our freedom of choice to participate in the I-don't-care-about-you society. We did that by extensively pursuing only our self-interest, and being indifferent to other people's suffering. Our system is primarily focused on our own financial wealth. In fact, it stimulates greed, and some people have even started to believe that greed is good. We learned to cheat other people with the intention of benefiting ourselves. Many people find this perfectly acceptable. However, by doing this, we have mistreated other people, and demonstrated a lack of respect for them. Don't think that this mistreatment of others only happens by others on a grand scale, and that we have no part in it. It happens on a small scale too, and we too might be involved in it somehow.

Apart from our dishonest behavior toward other people, we are also manhandling nature for our own short-term, self-interest. All of this is exactly the opposite of the nature of The Light, which is limitless and unconditional love for everyone and everything. As in a life review, we should become aware of our short sightedness and do something about it.

Thirdly, we should be genuinely sorry for our dishonest intentions toward each other, and for creating and sustaining this I-don't-care-about-you society. Moreover, we need to have the fundamental desire to change our behavior. This is like asking for some kind of forgiveness. To do this, we don't have to go around our city and beyond, ringing every doorbell. It suffices when we genuinely feel that we have been on the wrong track, and that we want to change. In fact, Alan Greenspan, the former president of the Federal Reserve, did something like that when in a congressional hearing. He honestly admitted that he was shocked to find out that the sole focus on self-interest does not work. Remember that, in a life review, The Light never becomes angry, even when we realize that we did something regrettable.

It is important that we choose the options that will increase love and energy in this world. Thus, we want to change the focus of our interest, and direct it to others and ourselves equally. Actually, it would be best if our focus would extend to a very important trinity. Apart from our neighbors and ourselves, it also involves The Light. We have to recognize that, in the unity universe, all three amount to the same thing.

Finally, we really have to make that change. The choice is ours. And the choice is individual. Each of us has to reconsider our function in the world. Each of us has the choice to start caring for others, and end our contribution to the I-don't-care-about-you society. At the very least, it means that we have to develop respect for each other, for the animal world, and nature as a whole. This means to have good intentions; to cherish integrity within ourselves and others; to be honest, incorruptible, and non-greedy; to allow others to have something we would like to have and still be genuinely happy for them; to be truly satisfied with the many things we have and to be grateful; to continuously create positive ripples. In short, we have to use our free will to become aligned with The Light.

The elderly lady who shared her candies with her school friend (see Chapter 2) told me that alignment makes her life easier. "When I open up to The Light or Universe, or whatever name one gives it, I feel more clearly what my task is. It becomes clearer about which direction to go. It gives me the feeling that I am in the right flow."

Another NDEr added something important. He stressed that this alignment with The Light is not a one-time event. "You should not only wonder whether you are aligned with The Light, but you have to ask that question regularly. Am I still aligned with The Light?"

Apparently, we can't just be satisfied and lean back after we think that we successfully aligned once. Getting aligned is a recurring process.

Make that change

Each of us has multiple tasks, such as caring for children, looking after parents, doing our jobs for which we get paid, running a business, or being part of a baseball team. Each of us also has one overarching task, which is the same for everyone: to bring love and harmony in this world, to expand our love, and to make it as big as possible. To enable us to fulfill our individual tasks, we are given talents, but also problems or challenges. We should do our utmost to use our talents well. We need to use them to perform our tasks as well as possible, and to tackle the problems in a positive way. We shouldn't cut corners. If we do, it is a form of dishonesty toward our employer, our customers, or our families, for example. In addition, we should strive for integrity and transparency. We should be honest and open about our intentions. The better our intentions are, the easier it is to be open and honest about them.

Of course, all of this also applies at higher collective levels. Families, clubs, companies, and governments should also strive for integrity and transparency. And again, when the intentions are good, it is easy for governments and companies to explain to the public what they do, and to be questioned about it.

It is important to be aware that we can make the world as we want it to be. Communism tried to force us into a certain direction, and it failed with disasterous results because it changed into dictatorship. Capitalism prescribed non-intervention so that self-interest would result in the most optimal allocation of resources, and create an optimum of wealth for everyone. The invisible hand would bring that about through free markets. Although it has brought us a lot of wealth, we presently have to acknowledge that pure capitalism has failed dearly. Never in history has there been a bigger destruction of wealth than we have witnessed during this Great Recession. We could have predicted this, because what else can we expect when short-term self-interest and indifference are the primary drivers? They lead to an I-don't-care about-you society.

This is precisely what we have to change. We have to take a next step in our development. We should expand our short-term self-interest to include everyone else's interest, and it should be a focus on the longer term. Consequently, we have to start focusing on our long-term "our-interest."

Long-term "our-interest"

This idea of long-term "our-interest" is something that follows from what many NDErs try to express. For instance, the quote at the end of Chapter 3: "Struggle and duality are a pitiful waste of energy. Love and unity and sharing will bring us joy, warmth, and being."

The child NDEr who was shown the future by his grandfather spoke about the imbalance in the world, which needs to be restored. He compared it with a human body that should be in balance to be healthy. He says, "Every cell in our body has a function and is in direct contact with other cells to be able to work together. Only in this way can the body function properly. The body is one huge cell machine, which we control with our consciousness." He concludes that, in the same way as cells in a body work together, we should communicate and work together in society. Society as a whole can only function properly in this way.

Interestingly, the elderly lady also used the comparison with cells in a body working together. She worries about people who ignore this profound interconnectedness and pretend it doesn't exist. Because there are so many of them, she feels that it will not take long before things will happen. She knows this for sure, but cannot precisely say what things will happen, or when. She says, "Everyone has an important task on earth, just like each cell in our body has a specific task. When a cell is not well-connected with other cells, it will become ill, or it will harm cells around it, or it will harm important bodily functions. When this happens with many cells, something such as cancer may even develop and, eventually the whole body will suffer. Likewise, every human being has a task, just like cells in a body, and one cannot just disconnect oneself from the whole, or ignore that there is a deep interconnection within universe. Only when people acknowledge their mutual interconnectedness, can the whole be sustained."

Focusing on our long-term "our-interest" would lead to a sustainable capitalism. In this kind of capitalism, we would still be free to make choices, but would voluntarily also take into consideration how our choices would affect others, and we would be concerned about the depletion of natural resources, the climate change, and the scarcity of water. We wouldn't be indifferent at all to others and nature, because we would wish to be in harmony with both. We would have an eye for people in need, the poor people who are not able to meet their basic needs, and who are trapped in poverty. We would make sure they would have sufficient means to improve themselves. We would all benefit from our changed attitude.

"Our-interest" would also mean that companies would have a sustainable, long-term strategy, taking into account that the availability of commodities is limited. When, for instance, car companies would have adopted such a strategy some decades ago, they wouldn't be languishing now. Instead, they would have put more effort in developing more advanced cars that pollute less and are more economical on gas (or probably wouldn't use gas at all). This could already have been reality when gas prices would have included an add-up for environmental costs long ago. We need more free-markets, but only those where prices correctly reflect all costs, including the non-financial ones.

If we would pursue our long-term "our-interest," we would steer our resources much more. We would collectively develop a vision on what we want to achieve. Where do we want to be in 10, 30, or 50 years? How do we want the earth to look at that time? What do we want society to be like in a few decades? These visions should be about all of us and all of nature. Then we can allocate our resources accordingly. In determining our vision, and the projects that are necessary to realize that vision, we must listen more to our spiritual nature. Our spiritual nature is interconnected, and cares in a universal way. It is not primarily focused on self-interest; on the contrary, it is interested in others as well, and in nature.

There is more than enough to do. Invest in a more efficient use of natural resources, notably oil, because their availability is clearly limited. If we don't do this, after this prolonged recession, when the economy picks up again, we will once more see a new oil price explosion. We will tumble in the same pit we just climbed out of. So, let's invest in clean and sustainable energy resources, in a clean environment, in healthcare, and in high quality education for everyone, which means investing in people.

And finally, with very high priority: We should invest in water. Even though the oceans are filled with it, there is a staggering increase in the lack of water. We should, for example, engage in more research on efficient ways to desalinate sea water. There are hundreds of millions of people who have no access to clean drinking water, and there are vast arid areas in the world that could be cultivated. In the long run, these investments would pay off tremendously. It could be one of the best investments in history. Obviously, any private company would be too small to embark on such a major project, but we can do it together, on a national, or even international level.

There is an important example of such a major project. Think of the wish to explore space, and to put a man on the moon. In the 1960s, it was possible to deliberately devote resources to that purpose instead of relying on the market to do it. Actually, at that time, it was too much for the market to handle. NASA was established, the investment was done, and men were put on the moon. After that, there were many other space activities, and they paid off. Think of the many products that make our lives easy, such as cell phones and GPS. And from space, we can monitor the shrinking of the ice caps more accurately.

The message in many NDEs concerning the urgent need to change should be seen as an "Emergency Call of Love," as one NDEr put it. "There is a different way of living and loving that does justice to ourselves, others, and the earth. We live on the edge of a number of crises that can give humanity a very rough time. Are we being shaken-up by so many who have seen a reality that far supersedes our reality? It seems like it: the NDE as an Emergency Call of Love."

In these times, we are faced with some great challenges, both financially and environmentally, but we should know that we can handle them. However, we cannot do that alone. We have to help each other. We can only do it together. When we recognize this truth, and become more aligned with The Light, we will be able to come through. The result will be wonderful.

The woman who foresaw the Great Recession in her NDE is confident about our ability to meet these challenges.

"Free will? Yes absolutely. We can choose. We can direct with our thoughts. That is why we should consistently think it will be alright. There really will be a better world. And when it is there, everyone will say, 'apparently, things can be different and better.'"

Become aligned with The Light

Becoming aligned with The Light doesn't mean that we have to start with sitting down several times a day, to meditate in a prescribed way. Meditating helps, and so does praying. But these are not the only ways to get into contact with The Light. Remember, The Light is very close by. Actually, It is part of us. It is within us. We just have to start realizing every day that we are participating in The Light, and that we are profoundly interconnected with all and everyone. Then, we must live up to that standard. This means that we must intend to act in a truly compassionate way, and to produce positive thoughts. This is healing for us and for the universe, because this creates the right ripples for increasing energy. If our intentions are right, we will be guided in the right direction. The alignment will come by itself, and we will become conscious of it. We will then go with the right flow. In fact, it's not difficult at all, but it will always be our choice whether we want to realize the connection with The Light in the first place. And remember, it is a recurring process.

So the sequence is: realize our participation in The Light and our interconnectedness with others and nature; intend to act compassionately and produce positive thoughts; alignment will be the result. In principle, it's very easy.

CHAPTER 10

ADVICE FOR NEW NDERS

"If you enter this world knowing you are loved and you leave this world knowing the same, then everything that happens in between can be dealt with."
~MICHAEL JACKSON[1]

If it wasn't for NDErs, this book you are holding would not be here. I had interviews with dozens of these courageous people. They are courageous because they choose to come back on earth, sometimes unwillingly, but they returned nonetheless, and continued living in this confining thing, this wet suit that is our body. In addition, they have to cope with many other restrictions in our imperfect four-dimensional world, the most important imperfection being the tremendous lack of love.

On average, it takes about seven years before NDErs find a way to live with their experience and to integrate it into their lives. However, the longing for that other world never really goes away. It will always be there. Also, for people who had a distressful NDE, it takes a lot of time, possibly even more than seven years, before they can function normally in our world again. They too will have after-effects similar to those of people who had a positive NDE.

The experience doesn't only affect NDErs themselves, but also their loved ones, and other people close to them. Because I felt the deep pain of NDErs and their loved ones, I asked seasoned experiencers what advice they would have for people who have recently had an NDE. It could help these newcomers with blissful, distressful, or mixed NDEs (and those close to them) cope and somehow shorten the period of integration. And it may help people who will have such an experience in the future. It might be you, even if you already had one, because each new experience is so overwhelming, that it needs to be integrated all over again.

Shortening the period in which people need to integrate their experience in their lives would not only be beneficial to them, but also to the world at large. I thoroughly believe that people with an NDE can help improve this world by being open about their experience and use it for the benefit of everyone who comes their way. There is a lot of wonderful work to do, and the funny thing is, the advice to do this work can very well be followed by non-NDErs, too.

Homesickness

"I don't want to be here" is a typical thing for NDErs to say, even years after their experience. Often, people around the NDEr do not know how to react or what to do. It sometimes starts just after the experience, when nurses and doctors are not able to respond correctly. There are many stories in which they react angrily after a patient comes round and expresses disappointment at being alive. Imagine how it is for doctors and nurses to have given their utmost to rescue someone from death, and then not feeling any gratitude at all for their hard work. Nevertheless, they have to learn to react with understanding, because that is the first thing NDErs need.

"I cried a lot." "I cried for weeks." "I was not really complete here." "I wanted to go back home to that wonderful place where I belong." "The event drove me crazy." These are just a few quotes that show how difficult it is for NDErs to come back again. Even many years after the experience, some still become emotional when they talk about it, or when they think back to what they have seen and felt. It is a kind of homesickness that never really wears off. The longing is there every day. It may become manageable, but it is definitely there to stay.

At first, there is generally a very clear feeling of happiness of having experienced this wonderful world, and having had amazing and expanded insights in life, and everything there is to know. Because they experienced the unlimited vastness of love, their own capacity for love expanded and seemed to have no limits any longer. Love started to burn within them.

One said that energy flowed very easily through her, and that her senses became very clear. She became amazed by every little detail. Another one was impressed by the movements of her hands and what they were capable of. Someone else was awed by the small animals in her garden. "Hello snail…beautiful butterfly." She clearly saw the beauty in everything, and for a long time, she was up in the clouds. In general, all NDErs are euphoric about the wonders of the world we live in. Non-NDErs would do well to appreciate these wonders as well.

They often want to share this euphoric feeling with all other human beings. They need to find a way to express this burning love within them. Some seem to float through the city, and just want to kiss everybody. One NDEr said, "I walked around as a saint. It was two weeks of bliss. I went to sex shops, drug bins, grocery stores to tell people that God loves them."

After those two weeks, reality kicked in. He discovered that not everyone felt the same way, and that most people didn't want to be bothered. He rapidly tumbled into a deep depression, which lasted for two months. He didn't dare to go out anymore, because he could feel everyone's energy. He knew what other people were thinking, and how they were thinking. Many other NDErs follow a similar pattern. One even withdrew into herself, and retreated to the room in the attic for almost one whole year, only to come out to do things of the utmost necessity.

NDErs also have important after-effects.[2] Some of them were already mentioned, such as no fear of death, a universal feeling of love, a greater tolerance for everyone, and problems with time. But money and social status also lose their importance. They become less religious, yet more spiritual. They often have clearer senses. Noise can be difficult to cope with: stirring a teaspoon in a cup can be hell, just like the rustling of a newspaper. The sounds just hammer their way through their heads. Sunglasses may become an absolute necessity, because they often feel that light is too bright. They should be careful with taking medicine, because the normal dose could already be too much.

In Chapter 2, it was explained that NDErs keep an open connection with that other part of the unity universe. The door to the other world is ajar, which means that they can still have experiences that are unfamiliar in our four-dimensional mechanical world. Sometimes they have a very clear intuitive feeling. Even a heightened sense of smelling and hearing were reported.

One occasionally heard a voice saying the wisest things. There is a finely honed sensitivity or, rather, a paranormal sensitivity, which enables some to predict the future.

Interestingly, this heightened sensitivity also seems to be picked up by non-NDErs. They feel that there is something trustworthy and non-judgmental about NDErs, even though they don't know them. Many NDErs have the experience that complete strangers start talking to them about their problems or their inner-most feelings.

All after-effects make NDErs different from who they previously were. They no longer fit in well. They have trouble to find their place in society again. They sometimes long so much for that delightful feeling, that they seem to isolate themselves from their environment.

We should especially take care of children who have had an NDE. They turn silent and withdraw into their own world. They often will see things that we don't see, and if they try to tell us about it, we should take them seriously. If we don't, and laugh them away, we jeopardize our contact with the child. In fact, we should take all children serious, because they are still more sensitive to that other world than adults are. Life, and learning that our ego exists, have a restricting effect on our senses for that other world. Our senses have become polluted, so to speak.

Advice from seasoned experiencers

It is useless to try to forget your experience. The more you try, the bigger it becomes. So if people tell you to let it go, explain to them that many have tried, but failed completely. They found out the hard way that it's impossible to ignore their experience.

The prime advice seasoned experiencers give is to express yourself. Be open about your experience. Talk about it! Read about it! Write it down! Seek other experiencers, and exchange feelings with them.

At the very least, try to talk to your partner. Your partner should listen. You have changed thoroughly, and partners have to realize that this is irreversible. Not being able to keep up with the change or, worse, not accepting it, may lead to the end of the relationship. As a matter of fact, many NDErs have gone through divorces.

A divorce is avoidable. Moreover, there can be a sunny side for your partner, too. Your change is there to stay, and it isn't easy for your partner to try to cope with, but it is worth the effort. There may be a wonderful reward: Both of you will grow in an unprecedented way. This can be very fulfilling for both, and for many more.

One partner of an NDEr said that his wife's NDE gave him opportunities to grow as well.[3] He discovered that trying to understand his wife, and the feelings that she went through, eventually made him more aware of the importance of empathy, self-esteem, and self-acceptance.

He said that knowledge is power, and that is why he fully informed himself on this topic. He read a great deal about NDEs to understand the phenomenon, and to understand her.

This enabled him to not only listen carefully to her with an open mind, but also to react to what she said in a way that she could relate to. And in turn, she listened to him.

He also advises to trust life and to rely on universe for the right direction. That is something NDErs say as well: Trust that you will be helped, and that things will go as they are supposed to go. Some parts of our lives can be quite difficult, but then when we come through, we will rejoice that we learned the lessons they held.

In addition, he said it is important to take care of oneself by talking about it to a trustworthy other, and to relax sufficiently. After all, the whole process consumes loads of energy. It was a difficult time for both, because the NDE dominated their lives. They found a way to live with it, and now he is grateful that they managed to hang in there. Even though he didn't have an NDE himself, he says that he is permeated by it. He feels he is able to reap the same fruits from an NDE as his wife.

The most important fruit is that NDErs start to have feelings of love for everything and everyone. This burning feeling does not go away. To some people, often the partner, this may seem threatening, but they have to understand that the increased feelings of love are not of a personal kind. It is not a love directed at one person, or even at a few people. It is the kind of love that is more universal, which also includes the love for nature.

Even though NDErs know the paramount importance of love, it should be noted that NDErs are no saints. They are still human beings with their own limitations. Of course, they realize that they are light, but they sometimes forget that this light is still contained in matter. It is restricted by it. They struggle to find the most loving way to react to whatever happens in their lives, and just like anyone else who tries, sometimes they fail miserably. But in the end good, intentions count.

When you talk with others about your experience, realize that many people still think that these are hallucinations. There are even doctors and nurses that hold that belief. Point to research previously mentioned in this book, and tell them that mainstream medical science has acknowledged these experiences as real. Strictly speaking, from a scientific point of view, the real cause of an NDE is still not known, but many assumed causes were ruled out. It was established, for example, that NDEs are not caused by physiological changes in the brain (such as brain cells dying, or a deficient supply of oxygen to the brain), pharmacological factors (medication), or psychological reactions to approaching death. In any case, the experience is there and there are millions of people with similar experiences.

Be conscious of the people you talk to. There are people who are rooted in fundamentalist beliefs. Religious people often don't have an open mind. In some cases, they have told NDErs that their experience is from the devil, or worse. I would like to ask them how that is possible when the NDErs have the wish to focus on love in the broadest way, and start being focused on long-term "our-interest."

One NDEr also advised to talk with commonsensical people. It is not as if people who lean heavily towards mysticism are no good, but you also need to ground yourself. You need to reconnect with earth, and manage the time you spend up in the clouds. The reason is very simple: You have things to do on earth. That is why you haven't completely died. There is a purpose for you being here, as there is a purpose for everyone, including non-NDErs. Behold the truth of this sentence: It's a biggie.

Homesickness can spoil your life and make it more difficult to fulfill your purpose on earth, because it can act like a trap. So, do things to feel your body again, such as fitness and sports. Take walks, go cycling, and preferably with others. Take dancing lessons, or express yourself and your body in another way. Or do something with earth. Put your hands in it, literally. Start gardening or molding clay. Or do something artistic, such as painting, drawing, knitting, or anything artistic. Redecorate your home or someone else's. You can also become aware of your body through yoga, and a step further would be meditation, when you concentrate on the physical process of breathing.

An important part of the integration process is to learn to cope with time as we know it here on earth. Here, time passes by, and for that reason, it forms one of the major limitations in our lives. It requires us to plan and organize—something NDErs have difficulty with.

All of this is necessary to start living in your body again, and to enjoy it for as long as it will be your temporary home. Reconnecting to the material world is necessary, because you need balance. It will remain easy for you to get in touch with that other part of the unity universe, to feel energies that are not of our four-dimensional world, and some of you may even be able to escape your body temporarily. Remember, the door to that other world is ajar. But you should also realize that when it is not your time, it will not be open enough to escape completely.

Your life will never be as it was before, but don't be afraid. You will learn to manage, and there will be help if you truly wish for it.

Too much openness

After an NDE, you have to be aware of your open channel to the other world. And be aware that, in principle, it is open for all sorts of vibrations and energies, also for the sort you don't want to get in contact with. It's a channel that uninvited guests can use. Therefore, stay in charge, and focus on The Light. And most of all, don't be afraid.

Fortunately, most people will discover that the channel is used by the light side of the unity universe. If you allow it to happen, this light side will be able to work miracles through you. You will be able to help others and yourself. This will not immediately be the case, and it will take time to evolve and develop. It's a very interesting learning process which can bring a lot of joy. Nevertheless, in a few cases, NDErs have seen negative darkness trying to interfere with them. To some extent, this interference was successful, but eventually didn't work out, because there was always help. Sometimes help arrives in unexpected ways.

Remember the story of Desirée in Chapter 5. After her experience, she was extremely open. She left her body regularly, and then seemed not to fit into it again. Negative darkness even tried to prevent her from returning to her body.

Betty Eadie also wrote about horrific creatures trying to attack her when she was lying in the hospital bed, recovering from her operation during which she had her NDE. They appeared half-human and half-animal. They had long claws and hateful faces, and approached her, hissing and growling. She was too weak or too paralyzed with fear to move, and she was sure she would fall victim to these creatures. Suddenly, a sort of dome of light covered her and the creatures couldn't reach her anymore.

In other examples I came across, the dark energy didn't attack the NDEr directly, as in the cases of Desirée or Betty, but resorted to sly tricks to harm them. It is very easy to mislead NDErs when they are still confused by their experience. They are easy targets, especially when they are still in a state of euphoria, and are still very open and trusting. Negative darkness can take disguising forms like a voice that speaks in a reassuring way. It tries to persuade NDErs to do things that would not only harm others, but, more importantly, themselves. I was explicitly told by these NDErs that the True Light or true light beings would never ask someone to do anything that would be harmful to anyone. And *anyone* explicitly includes themselves: NDErs would never be asked to do anything that would harm themselves. Remember, The Light is unconditional love. In addition, It allows us to make our own choices, because through our choices we have the ability to show our love, and that is what it is all about. Consequently, The Light would never pressure us to do anything. And if It would ask us to do something, it would be only something lovely. Therefore, we should never feel obliged to do anything, which we think is not aligned with love.

There is work to be done

Nice NDEs are wonderful and blissful, and all NDEs are overwhelming, revealing, confronting, and much more. However, that's not all there is to it. You have to do something with your experience. As one NDEr said, "An NDE is a lot of work! It is not a final destination. It is not only an ultimate experience, it's also the starting point of a lot of work."

You have to find out for yourself what its purpose is. That may not be easy, but there is no other choice than to try. One NDEr said, "It was wonderful, but I know I have to do something with it. To find out what that is exactly, is the most difficult thing in my life, and I don't always feel like trying."

There are a few obvious leads. An NDE is like winning a lottery: You've won a big treasure that will cause your life never to be the same again. There is more resemblance with having a treasure. You shouldn't store it in a mattress. Or to put it differently: Don't hide your light under a bushel. You have to do something productive with it.

An NDE makes you feel like being born again. You change thoroughly and get a different view of life. You'll think differently, talk differently, and live differently. Perhaps you'll even have specific after-effects. All of this cannot be ignored, and you must translate this into daily life. If your experience was a joyful one, then that is what you have to radiate. Send radiant, joyful ripples through the world around you. Find a way to express yourself. If your experience was not so joyful, know that The Light loves you anyway. And, for you, creating positive ripples is just as important as it is for anyone else.

One way to create joyful and positive ripples is to serve. Service is very powerful in bringing about happiness. It makes us happy, and it makes others happy. It binds the love in us. However, a word of caution is required when you use your open connection for the benefit of others. You should be careful with the energy you acquired. Don't just throw it around and spend it on everyone. If you do, you'll soon find yourself exhausted. Contain your energy, and don't feel responsible for everything you see or feel. For example, an NDEr who was a teacher could feel all the problems her pupils had at home. At times, that was too much for her. It wore her out. She needed to be told to close up, and realize that she cannot carry the weight of everyone's misery on her shoulders. That cannot be the purpose of anyone's life. So, be warned—and find balance.

In finding your way and your balance, you'll discover that things become easier when you get aligned with The Light. Doing this is very important. As one NDEr said, "An NDE is an invitation to partake in the work of The Light Power. It's like an invitation to dance."

Before we were born, we decided to participate in this work, and start on an adventure called life. Absolutely everything we experience in our life occurs to give us possibilities to choose and to develop compassion. In this way, we gain insight in the meaning of love. And the more we understand love, the closer we will come to understanding The Light. While an NDE can certainly make it possible to gain tremendous insight, there will always be a lot to learn and discover long after the experience is over. Christian Andréason said about himself and other NDErs, "Yes, you may have experienced a divine revelation, but life will keep revealing even more to you, especially later on, as you maintain the courage to keep living it! I am always amazed at just how much I have maintained the process of learning from my own NDE, even after all these years. While it is true that Heaven revealed a lot to me, I find that I am still putting all the pieces together and probably will be for the rest of my life."

The nice thing is that you'll get the energy needed to do that entire discovery. An NDEr said that throughout the years, she became aware that the energy that she had felt during her NDE became integrated in her life more and more. She feels that wonderful energy daily. This energy will get you through.

It can rejuvenate you. "It is more generative than degenerative." It is an energy that is available for everyone. You just have to learn how to effectively tap into it. Being aligned with The Light is very helpful.

And the nicest thing about this advice is that it applies not only to NDErs, but to other people as well. There is work enough for everyone to do. Start by getting aligned!

Notes

Epigraph

1. For more poems by Frans Tomeij, see: *www.naturalhealingcenter.com/mmp.htm.*

Chapter 1

1. Dubbed "Great Implosion" by Roger Bootle.

Chapter 2

1. For a good overview of the field of NDEs, see Atwater (2007), Holden c.s., or Van Lommel.

2. See for instance Murphy or Kellehear (2001) and (2008).

3. IANDS is the International Association for Near-Death Studies see *www.iands.org*.

4. See for instance Fenwick and Fenwick, pp. 154 and 159 and Perry, p.130.

5. NDE submitted to the publically accessible IANDS archives (*www.iands.org/nde_archives/*) where it was first published on Tuesday, November 11, 2003; 4:39 p.m. (also *Monthly NDE*, May 2008).

6. Ring and Cooper.

7. Ring and Cooper, p. 135.

8. NDE submitted to the publically accessible IANDS archives (*www.iands.org/nde_archives/*) where it was first published on Thursday, March 25, 2004; 9:14 p.m. (also *Monthly NDE*, June 2007).

9. NDE submitted to the publically accessible IANDS archives (*www.iands.org/nde_archives/*) where it was first published on Thursday, March 25, 2004; 9:14 p.m. (also *Monthly NDE*, June 2007).

10. Taylor, p. 140.

11. Taylor, pp. 73 and 137.

12. Tienke Klein, p. 246.

13. NDE submitted to the publically accessible IANDS archives (*www.iands.org/nde_archives/*) where it was first published on Thursday, March 25, 2004; 9:14 p.m. (also *Monthly NDE*, June 2007).

14. NDE submitted to the publically accessible IANDS archives (*www.iands.org/nde_archives/*) where it was first published with the title "Three accounts" (also *Monthly NDE*, October 2006).

15. NDE submitted to the publically accessible IANDS archives (*www.iands.org/nde_archives/*) where it was first published on Thursday, March 25, 2004; 9:14 p.m. (also *Monthly NDE*, June 2007).

16. Blackmore, pp. 127–128. This incident has been extensively discussed in the *Journal of Near-Death Studies*, Volume 25, number 4, Summer 2007.

17. See Smit. Rudolf H. Smit took the initiative to corroborate the dentures anecdote, which he did with the help of Titus Rivas and Anny Dirven. The first interview with the "NDEr with the dentures" was by Ap Addink.

18. Sabom, 37–52; BBC.

19. Hawking, p. 155.

20. Also see the movie *Down the Rabbit Hole*, the follow-up of *What the Beep Do We Know*.

21. Kübler-Ross, 1969 and 1975 en Moody, 1975 en 1976.

22. See also Callanan and Kelly, pp. 38–55.

23. Van Lommel et al. See also Van Lommel.

24. Parnia et al, Schwaninger et al and Sartori.

25. Greyson (2003), in this study there was, for example, no interview after eight years.

26. Greyson (2007), p. 242. See also Fenwick, p. 150.

Chapter 3

1. Her story was published in a very interesting book *De tweede helft*, by Ditta op den Dries. This is a book about the life of NDErs after their experience, so to speak the second half of their lives. It shows how NDErs cope with their experiences.

2. Cox-Chapman, p. 80.

3. Burton, p. 14.

4. Klein, p. 105.

5. NDE submitted to the publically accessible IANDS archives (*www.iands.org/nde_archives/*) where it was first published with the title "Shimmering River of Life" (also *Monthly NDE,* March 2007).

6. Quran, Sura 50:16.

7. Klein.

8. Interview by Z.J. Gilze with Tienke Klein in a Dutch magazine *Mijn Geheim*, pp. 48–54.

9. Interview by Z.J. Gilze with Tienke Klein in a Dutch magazine *Mijn Geheim*, p. 53.

10. NDE submitted to the publically accessible IANDS archives (*www.iands.org/nde_archives/*) where it was first published on Tuesday, July 1, 2003; 11p.m. (also *Monthly NDE,* January 2008).

11. Storm, p. 73.

12. Storm, p. 73.

13. Storm, p. 42.

Chapter 4

1. Burton, p. 14.

2. NDE submitted to the publically accessible IANDS archives (*www.iands.org/nde_archives/*) where it was first published on Thursday, March 25, 2004; 9:14 p.m. (also *Monthly NDE,* June 2007).

3. NDE submitted to the publically accessible IANDS archives (*www.iands.org/nde_archives/*) where it was first published on Friday, November 28, 2003; 10:36 a.m. (also *Monthly NDE,* June 2008).

4. NDE submitted to the publically accessible IANDS archives (*www.iands.org/nde_archives/*) where it was first published with the title "Three accounts" (also *Monthly NDE,* October 2006).

5. The CD or audio download of the panel: "NDEs and Suicide" can be obtained through the IANDS Website (*www.iands.org/conferences/2006/panel_ndes_and_suicide.html*). His story was also published in *When Ego Dies*, with a foreword by Dian Corcoran.

6. Futrell, p. 9.

7. Storm, pp. 38-41.

8. Suleman, p. 21.

9. Burrows, p. 5.

10. NDE submitted to the publically accessible IANDS archives (*www.iands.org/nde_archives/*) where it was first published on Thursday, March 4, 2004–08:58 p.m. (also *Monthly NDE,* July 2007).

11. See also Eadie.

Chapter 5

1. For more poems by Frans Tomeij, see: *www.naturalhealingcenter.com/mmp.htm.*

2. Burrows, p. 3-6.

3. Burrows, p. 5.

4. Klein, p. 206.

Chapter 6

1. For more about Christian Andréason, his music, and private one-on-one practice go to: *www.ChristianAndreason.com.*

2. For instance in Eadie, pp. 93–99, see also previous chapter with the story of Desirée.

3. Tienke Klein, pp. 185–189, 197–227, 249–250.

4. NDE submitted to the publically accessible IANDS archives (*www.iands.org/nde_archives/*) where it was first published with the title "Shimmering river of life" (also *Monthly NDE,* March 2007).

5. NDE submitted to the publically accessible IANDS-archives (*www.iands.org/nde_archives/*) where it was first published on Thursday, March 4, 2004; 8:58 p.m. (also *Monthly NDE,* July 2007).

6. Christian Andréason's story can be read in his forthcoming book, *Remembering Heaven* where an excerpt can be read on his Website: *www.ChristianAndreason.com.*

7. Eadie.

Chapter 7

1. A British psychic, who wrote this in one of her inspiring letters to me.

2. Distressful NDEs were described by Atwater (1992), Bonenfant, Van Lommel, Grey, Ring, Storm, Fenimore.

3. Futrell, p. 9.

4. Storm, pp. 10-18.

5. Storm, p. 21-23, 102.

6. Storm, p. 101.

7. Bush, p. 110.

8. Rommer, p. 26.

9. Atwater (1995), p. 49.

10. Awater (1992), p. 156.

11. Ring, p. 22.

12. Suleman, p.28.

13. Storm, pp. 52-54, 59, 108.

14. Her NDE has been described in detail in van Lommel, pp 191–206.

15. NDE submitted to the publically accessible IANDS archives (*www.iands.org/nde_archives/*) where it was first published on Tuesday, March 30, 2004; 9:55 p.m. (also *Monthly NDE,* October 2008).

16. Ring and Franklin, p. 206.

17. Futrell, p. 9. In chapter 4, near note 6, there is the original quote and some additional comment.

18. Rommer, p. 26.

19. Mark Giordani's Journey, p. 5. Also listen to *www.inspiredaudio.com*

20. Ritchie, p. 47–67, Fenimore.

21. Storm, pp. 19–29.

Chapter 8

1. Dubbed "Great Implosion" by Roger Bootle.

2. Storm, p. 44

3. Kaufman, p.222.

4. Estimation by the UN for 2007.

5. Bootle, Roger, p. 247.

6. OECD Environmental Outlook 2008, Paris.

7. See *www.copenhagenclimatecouncil.com.* See also *www. ipcc.ch* for more about the Intergovernmental Panel on Climate Change. The March 2009 scientific congress preceded the U.N. Climate Change Conference, also in Copenhagen, where a watered down Climate Accord (the Copenhagen Accord) was adopted and is now supposed to be the first step toward a better climatologically environment.

Chapter 9

1. See also chapter 4.

2. See László and Van Lommel.

Chapter 10

1. See Brainy Quote: *http://www.brainyquote.com/quotes/ quotes/m/michaeljac403017.html*

2. More about after-effects see, for instance, Atwater (1995).

3. This was taken from the lecture that Henk-Jan van der Veen gave on September 26, 2009, for a congress of

Merkawah, the Dutch division of IANDS. The topic of the lecture was coping with the NDE of your partner in which he elaborated on his experience with being the husband of an NDEr.

BIBLIOGRAPHY

Atwater, P.M.H. "Is There a Hell? Surprising Observations About the Near-Death Experience." *Journal of Near-Death Studies* 10:3 (1992).

———. *The Big Book of Near-Death Experiences.* Newburyport, Mass.: Hampton Roads Publishing Company, 2007.

Blackmore, Susan J. *Dying to Live: Near-Death Experiences.* Buffalo, N.Y.: Prometheus, 1993.

Bonenfant, Richard J. "A Child's Encounter with the Devil. An Unusual Near-Death Experience with Both Blissful and Frightening Elements." *Journal of Near-Death Studies* 20:2 (2001): 87–100.

Bootle, Roger. *The Trouble with Markets; Saving Capitalism from Itself.* London, Boston: Nicholas Brealey Publishing, 2009.

Broome, Kate. "The Day I Died." *BBC/TLC* (2002).

Burrows, Bonni J. "My journey trough a doorway called death (part two)." *Vital Signs* (Publication of IANDS) 24:1 (2005): 3–6.

Burton, Catherine. "Counseling from a Near-Death Perspective." *Vital Signs* (Publication of IANDS) 21:1 (2002/2003): 5–15.

Bush, Nancy Evans. "Afterward: Making Meaning After a Frightening Near-Death Experience." *Journal of Near-Death Studies* 21:2 (2002): 99–133.

Callanan, Maggie, and Patricia Kelly. *Final Gifts, Understanding the Special Awareness, Needs, and Communications of the Dying.* New York: Bantam Books, 1997.

Corcoran, Diane. *When Ego Dies: A Compilation of Near-Death & Mystical Conversion Experiences* (foreword). Hot Spring National Park, Ark.: Emerald Ink Publishing, 1996.

Cox-Chapman, Mally. *The Case for Heaven.* New York: G.P. Putnam's Suns, 1995.

Eadie, Betty J. *Embraced By the Light, 3rd edition.* Placerville, Calif.: Gold Leaf Press, 1994.

Fenimore, Angie. *Beyond the Darkness.* New York: Bantam Books, 1995.

Fenwick, Peter. "Science and Spirituality: A Challenge for the 21st Century." *Journal of Near-Death Studies*. 23:3 (2005) 131–157.

Fenwick, Peter, and Elizabeth Fenwick. *The Truth in the Light: An Investigation of Over 300 Near-Death Experiences*. New York: Berkley Books, 1997.

Futrell, Michellena. "Not Afraid of Death—But Not Allowed to Die." *Vital Signs* (Publication of IANDS) 22:2 (2003): 3, 8–9.

Gilze, Z.J. "'Boven' is dichterbij dan we denken." *Mijn geheim*, 4 March 2008, 48–54.

Giordani, Mark. "Mark Giordani's Journey." *Vital Signs* (Publication of IANDS) 21:2 (2002): 5–18.

Grey, Margot. *Return from the Death: An Exploration of Near-Death Experience*. London, Boston: Arcana, 1985.

Greyson, Bruce. "Incidence and correlates of near-death experiences in a cardiac care unit." *General Hospice Psychiatry* 25:4 (2003): 269–276.

———. Comments on "Does Paranormal Perception Occur in Near-Death Experiences?" *Journal of Near-Death Studies* 25:4 (2007): 237–244.

Hawking, Stephen W. *The Theory of Everything, The Origin and Fate of the Universe*. Beverly Hills, Calif.: New Milennium Press, 2002.

Holden, C.S., Janice Miner, Bruce Greyson, and Debbie James. *The Handbook of Near-Death Experiences*. Santa Barbara, Calif.: 2009.

Kaufman, Henry. *The Road to Financial Reformation; Warnings, Consequences, Reforms*. Hoboken, N.J.: John Wiley & Sons, 2009.

Kellehear, Allan. "A Hawaiian Near-Death Experience." *Journal of Near-Death Studies* 20:1 (2001): 31–35.

——— . "Census of Non-Western Near-Death Experiences to 2005: Overview of the Current Data." *Journal of Near-Death Studies* 26:4 (2008): 249–265.

Klein, Tienke. *De Kiem.* Barchem, NL: Uitgeverij Petiet, 2006.

Kübler-Ross, Elisabeth. *Death, the Final Stage of Growth.* Saddle River, N.J.: Prentice Hall, 1975.

——— . *On Death and Dying* New York: Macmillan Books, 1969.

László, Ervin. *The Akashic Field.* New York: Penguin, 2007.

op den Dries, Ditta. *De tweede helft. Hoe een Bijna-Dood Ervaring levens verandert.* Kampen, NL: Uitgeverij Ten Have, 2009.

Organization for Economic Cooperation and Development (OECD) "Reconciling Development and Environmental Goals: Measuring the Impact of Policies." *OECD.* Paris, 2008.

Parnia, Sam, D.G. Waller, R. Yeates, and P. Fenwick. "A qualitative and quantitative study of the incidence, features and aetiology of near-death experiences in cardiac arrest survivors." *Resuscitation* 48:2 (2001): 149–156.

Moody, Raymond A. *Life After Life.* Covington, Ga.: Mockingbird Books, 1975.

——— . *Reflections on Life After Life.* Covington, Ga.: Mockingbird Books, 1976.

Murphy, Todd. "Near-Death Experiences in Thailand." *Journal of Near-Death Studies* 19:3 (2001): 161–178.

Ring, Kenneth. "Solving the Riddle of Frightening Near-Death Experiences: Some Testable Hypotheses and a Perspective Based on 'A Course in Miracles.'" *Journal of Near-Death Studies* 13:1 (1994): 5–23.

Ring, Kenneth, and Sharon Cooper. "Near-Death and Out-of-Body Experiences in the Blind: A Study of Apparent Eyeless Vision." *Journal of Near-Death Studies* 16:2 (1997): 101–147.

Ring, Kenneth, and Stephen Franklin. "Do Suicide Survivors report Near-Death Experiences?" *Omega* 12:3 (1981–82): 191–208.

Ritchie, George G. *Return from Tomorrow, 33rd ed.* Waco, Tex.: Chosen Books, 1978.

Rommer, Barbara R. *Blessing in Disguise.* St. Paul, Minn.: Llewellyn Publications, 2002

Sabom, M.B. *Light and Death: One Doctor's Fascinating Account of Near-Death Experiences.* Grand Rapids, Mich.: Zondervan Publishing House, 1998.

Sartori, Penny. "A long-term prospective study to investigate the incidence and phenomenology of Near-Death Experiences in a Welsh Intensive Therapy Unit." *IANDS.* iands. org/research. 2003.

Schwaninger, Janet, Paul R. Eisenberg, Kenneth B. Schechtman and Alan N. Weiss. "A Prospective Analysis of Near-Death Experiences in Cardiac Arrest Patients." *Journal of Near-Death Studies* 20:4 (2002): 215–232.

Smit, Rudolf H. "Corroboration of the Dentures Anecdote Involving Veridical Perception in a Near-Death Experience." *Journal of Near-Death Studies* 27:1 (2008) 47–61.

Storm, Howard. *My Descent into Death: A Second Chance at Life.* New York: Doubleday, 2005.

Suleman, Azmina. *A Passage to Eternity.* Calgary, Alberta: Amethyst Publishing, 2004.

Taylor, S. M. (2001). *Near-Death Experiences: Discovering and Living in Unity.* Dissertation Abstracts International, 63 (09), 3246A. (UMI No. 764829341).

van Lommel, P. *Consciousness Beyond Life. The Science of the Near-Death Experience.* New York: HarperOne, 2010.

van Lommel, P., R. van Wees, V.Meyers and I. Elfferich. "Near-death experience in survivors of cardiac arrest: a prospective study in the Netherlands." *The Lancet* 358 (2001): 2039–2045.

INDEX

211

About
the Author

Christophor Coppes holds a PhD in economics and worked for many years at the University of Groningen and in the banking industry. He was both in a commercial position with a French bank, as well as in a supervisory role at the Dutch Central Bank. Currently, he is still working for this institution, monitoring the developments in the international financial markets.

During his career in the financial sector, he never lost his human interest. This resulted in writing a book based on the real story of how friends and family lovingly looked after a terminally ill AIDS patient, and helped him through the final stages of his life.

In 1995, his disgust over the biggest single massacre in Europe after World War II in Srebrenica, made him write a book about the real experiences of one of the victims, a Muslim girl who became translator for the Dutch U.N. soldiers.

His conviction that Near-Death Experiences are true spiritual experiences dates back to 1979, when he read Raymond Moody's *Life after Life*. A few years ago, he wrote a book in which he compared the essences of NDEs with those of the five world religions. His conclusion is that the true essences of the five religions can be found in NDEs, but that not all the essences of NDEs can be found in each individual religion. In 2008, he became president of the International Association for Near-Death Studies (IANDS) in the Netherlands.

Christophor demonstrates his social engagement through his work as board member of the Society for Worldwide Dentistry. He participated in dental projects for underprivileged school children in Kenya and Cambodia. He lives in Amsterdam, the Netherlands.

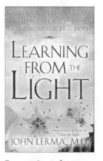

Also from NEW PAGE BOOKS

Science Was Wrong
Startling Truths About Cures, Theories, and Inventions "They" Declared Impossible
Stanton T. Friedman, MSc., and Kathleen Marden
EAN 978-1-60163-047-6
$15.99

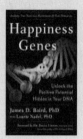

Happiness Genes
Unlock the Positive Potential Hidden in Your DNA
James D. Baird, PhD, with Laurie Nadel, PhD
EAN 978-1-60163-105-3
$15.99

Cosmic Conversations
Dialogues on the Nature of the Universe and the Search for Reality
Stephan Martin
EAN 978-1-60163-077-3
$16.99

History Is Wrong
Eric von Daniken
EAN 978-1-60163-086-5
$17.99

To order, call **1-800-227-3371** or go to **NewPageBooks.com**